SURVIVAL KIT

Other Books by Susan B. Anthony

Sobriety of the Heart

The Ghost in My Life

The Prayer-Supported Apostle

Treat Yourself to Life (Written with
  Dr. Raymond Charles Barker)

Women During the War and After,
  with Dr. Ann Shyne

Out of the Kitchen—Into the War

Cover photograph for *Survival Kit* by Larry Dunmire

YOU ARE NOT ALONE

Yet how often you think you are.

For when you are in despair, when you are hovering on the brink of nothingness, it seems there is nothing that can touch you, help you, save you.

But there is hope. You can survive. You can break through from suffering to sanity and even serenity in this chaotic world.

SURVIVAL KIT gives you the tools to transcend— to rise above and overcome your suffering—by making contact with God, with fellow human beings, with the world around you.

You are not alone. And you will survive.

Dr. Susan B. Anthony's
SURVIVAL KIT

Anthony, Susan Brownell, 1916-
    Survival Kit.

        1. Conduct of life.   2. Anthony, Susan Brownell,
1916-   . I. Title.
BJ1581.2.A57   1981   248.8'6   81-9771
ISBN 0-89638-050-5   AACR2

Grateful acknowledgment is made to the following for permission to quote from the works listed.

Alcoholics Anonymous Publishing, Inc., for *Alcoholics Anonymous,* 1955.

Catholic Action Office, for *The Prayer-Supported Apostle* by Susan B. Anthony, 1965.

Chosen Books, for *The Ghost in My Life* by Susan B. Anthony, 1971, 1979.

E. P. Dutton & Co., Inc., for a selection from the book *Mysticism* by Evelyn Underhill. Published in 1961 in the U.S.A. by E. P. Dutton & Co., Inc. in a paperback edition and used with their permission; and for a selection from *Man and the Supernatural* by Evelyn Underhill. Copyright, 1928 by E. P. Dutton & Co., Inc. Renewal, 1956, by H. Stuart Moore. Published by E. P. Dutton & Co., Inc. and used with their permission.

Harper and Row, Publishers, Inc., for *The Hour of the Tiger* by Mme. Induk Pahk, 1965; and for *The Spiritual Life* by Evelyn Underhill, n. d.

The Missionary Society of St. Paul the Apostle in the State of New York, for *As the Spirit Leads Us,* edited by Kevin and Dorothy Ranaghan, 1971.

The National Catholic Reporter Publishing Company, copublished with Pilgrim Press and National Catholic Reporter, for *Creative Suffering, The Ripple of Hope* by Alan Paton et al., 1970.

Thomas E. Powers, for *First Questions on the Life of the Spirit* by Thomas E. Powers, 1959.

Acknowledgments

My gratitude goes to all those who have given me the tools for my own survival kit, and to those who have helped bring this book to publication, especially to Rosemary Jones, who has made excellent suggestions on the whole manuscript; to the South Florida Prayer Community; to the staff of the Deerfield Beach Public Library; to Miss Margaret Elliston of the Biscayne College Library in Miami, and to many others.

To the kinship of survivors and transcenders of suffering, ranging from my mother, to the One who redeemed suffering for us all.

Contents

Chapter 1

The Survival Kit

When asked on a television show how I would sum up my rather stormy personal history, I answered without even having to think:

"I have survived."

This I share with all men, women, and children who are alive today. That *we have survived to this present moment* on our fragile spaceship earth is the chief fact of our existence, and *the one for which we should be most grateful* in view of the hazards of our world. The interviewer's next question was:

"How?"

I answered, "I have a *survival kit*—a kit of tools that has helped me not only survive suffering—but in some cases transcend it."

Once you start using these tools you'll find that they achieve far more than you ever hoped for. I define the word "tool" as the dictionary does to mean "any device for doing or facilitating work." These tools are not only devices for facilitating survival, they will help you make a breakthrough from suffering to sanity in our chaotic world; to serenity; and if you ever used all of the tools all of the time, you would be on your way to sanctity, or at least to the surrender that is a mark of sanctity.

These tools were given to me freely by hundreds of men and women through the spoken and written word. Freely I am passing them on to you who may at this moment need them. To possess your own sur-

vival kit *there is but one prerequisite—that is a flicker
of hope*, a flicker sometimes as wavering and infin-
itesimal as a tiny match flame, but a flicker that has
not gone out. If you also have faith and love, you are
that much more forward; but when we are in a fight
to survive suffering, we often have nothing but that
little hope, that *frail flicker of a will to live.*

Hope is enough to begin with. I know because that
is all I had when I called for help. The help came first
from those in what I call the kinship of suffering. It included ordinary men and women like myself who
have survived some form of suffering: alcoholism,
neurosis, anxiety, or drugs. It also included the
millions of fellow sojourners on this spaceship earth,
sufferers from war's slaughter, starvation, homeless-
ness—widows, bereft mothers, orphans; and sufferers
from poverty and injustice, whatever their nationality, creed, race, or sex.

The kinship became even more personal when I met
a survivor from Auschwitz, the Nazi death camp,
Rabbi Isaac Neuman. I came to know several survivors from cancer—Dorrie, a friend, among them.
The kinship certainly includes one celebrated mother,
Mrs. Rose Kennedy, who transcended the loss of four
of her children, by assassination and other violent
deaths, and Mrs. Martin Luther King, whose husband
was murdered. Then there is my friend Sarah
Gainham who transcended the trauma of witnessing
the murder of her parents. And another friend who
was one of the century's leading specialists in surviving sheer physical suffering, the celebrated writer
John Howard Griffin. He not only survived twelve
years of blindness and two years of paralysis from the
hips down—and wrote the first of his books during

this siege—but subsequently survived many operations to put his face back together after it was destroyed by pigmentation injections. These he submitted to in order to pass as a Negro in the South while writing his book *Black Like Me*.

The kinship of suffering certainly embraces those who have transcended poverty, among them the Reverend and Mrs. Francis Cook, who, as they said, "preferred soupbones with children to T-bones without." The Cooks raised nine adopted children on virtually nothing. And it includes Fay, who has only just survived her alcoholism, her years on welfare, supervised at every turn by case workers and doctors or aides at a nursing home. It includes the young drug abuser trying to go straight. And it embraces a young Lutheran pastor, Dietrich Bonhoffer, who transcended the suffering of awaiting momentary execution by the Nazis, and helped us today to survive by writing his priceless letters from his jail cell and camp. It also includes a survivor very close to me, my own mother.

Without their heroic examples and the tools they offered me, I could not have survived my own suffering. I doubt if I would be alive even to write down my own little list of ordeals: alcoholism, and recovery; later, a nearly twenty-year siege that I call my captivity in the cold war, a capitivity without bars, but one that included interrogations, threatened lifetime exile from the United States, and innumerable major restrictions on my right to live, work, travel, and marry. Then there were my broken marriages, sterility, and a near-fatal accident. I list these only to qualify, not to complain. But during these events it consoled me to know that I shared the same century, the same planet, with these true heroes and heroines of the kinship. It gave me sufficient hope to try to emulate them, saying to myself, "If they can survive their far greater suffering, I can at least keep going."

Miraculously, I was able to start giving out the tools they gave me to those who came to me for help (see the end of this chapter for a list of the first tools). Their very need for the tools drew me out of the prison of my own self-concern. Now the kinship began to embrace not only the masters who had taught me, but the students who became my own children of the spirit. The expanding number of those who helped me and those who came to me for help then convinced me of a truth long unseen. It is that there is a universality of suffering as inexorable as the universality of mortality. *Nobody has a monopoly on suffering.* Yet when we are suffering, each of us adds isolation and a delusion of uniqueness to the original cause of suffering.

Parents think that nothing could be worse than their anguish over draft-age sons, or rebelling, runaway, drug-addicted children.

Children think nothing could be worse than the chaos and futility of the future, and their parents' lack of understanding.

The old think that nothing could be worse than their loneliness, the brevity of the time that is left.

The unemployed think nothing could be worse than their lack of paychecks and their loss of dignity.

The rich think nothing could be worse than a threat to their fortune.

Lovers think nothing could be worse than the end of the affair.

The sick think nothing could be worse than their pain and disease.

Neurotics think nothing could be worse than their anxieties, depressions, and panics.

We could all remove at one blow a major cause of suffering if we would only recognize that some of it is indigenous to the human condition, in every person and throughout the planet. Our suffering is rarely unique either in kind or degree. In fact, the solidarity of suffering is one of our greatest bonds with each other. When a mother sees a film of another mother trying to protect her baby from machine gun bullets, she almost forgets that the woman is not herself. It takes a lot of brainwashing to dull and depersonalize us and thus break up the solidarity of humanity in compassion for suffering, to box us into total solitary confinement, as though only we had troubles. Imprisoned in these cells of our own suffering, we often emerge only to try the panaceas thrown up by our society especially in America. These include the following:

You can wallow in suffering, claim martyrdom, immerse yourself in self-pity, and make a real career of suffering.

Or you can go to the other extreme and stoutly deny that suffering exists at all; deny, as some do, that it has any reality to hurt you. You can in a way steadfastly refuse to accept the fact that you have lost someone you loved, that you are destitute, that you have been jilted, or that your house has been burned down.

Or you can try to flee suffering altogether by insulating yourself in a fortress that shuts out involvement in love, hope, work; in other words, living itself.

Or you can go to the opposite pole and plunge into

a full-scale analysis of the causes, symptoms, effects, and future possibilities of your suffering.

But by far the most popular panacea for personal suffering offered in America is none of these. It is simply to blot out any and all suffering with readily available drugs such as alcohol, tranquilizers, barbiturates, marijuana, LSD, or heroin.

If you have exhausted yourself and have given up on these "cures," you may be ready to try some of the tools that have been handed to me by the kinship of suffering, the many. You may even be ready to receive some directly from the One.

Human help led me to *survive*; it could not lead me to *transcend suffering, that is, to rise above and beyond suffering*. The day came when I began receiving tools not only from my human friends, but from Another. Survival sentences floated into mind fully formed either when I was in a state of crisis or of solitary wonder or meditation. The words came while I was snorkeling, or glancing at the Southern Cross flung diagonally across the tropical sky. They came while I was riding in a subway on a hot August day, or staring at a brick wall across from my apartment, or walking among the black trees of a winter-white wood.

One day I realized that even the survival sentences as separate tools had not been enough to bring any kind of order, let alone peace, to my life. Yes, they had kept me sober. But no, they had not given me sustained surcease from other forms of suffering. The devils of dubious excitement had continued to attack me not only in my personal life, but in the shocking disasters I had to cover as a newspaper reporter. Was I for the rest of my life going to survive one crisis only to fall into another? Perhaps I needed not just survival tools; perhaps I needed something that would put all these tools—these parts—together, into a coherent whole. Perhaps I needed a *survival kit*.

I looked up "kit" in the dictionary. It said, "A set of instruments or equipment used for a specific purpose: *a survival kit.* . . ." I saw I had been collecting not just tools, but a *set* of tools, and that all together they comprised a survival kit. Excitedly I read on to see that the kit is also defined as "a collection of personal effects, especially for travel."

Travel where? Where was I going? Even if my separate saving sentences did form a set, a kit, what was their purpose beyond survival? For what journey's end did a survival kit equip me?

Then I remembered an experience from my college days, mentioned in my book *The Ghost in My Life* (Chosen Books, 1971). I had nearly flunked biology. I was totally baffled by all those seemingly boring little creatures—amoebae, frogs, and crawfish. To me they were just annoying trifles in a maze of microscopes, slides, and tweezers. Had I seen biology not as a series of unrelated objects and experiments, had I seen it as the orderly and majestic evolution of living matter from the simplest of single cells ascending to the complex and conscious goal we call a human being, I might well have excelled in biology.

Now it came to me that there just might be a similar evolution of the soul. Perhaps the inner self must undergo an evolution, just as does the biological entity. Perhaps suffering was part of that growth. Perhaps suffering forced some kind of awakening, and awakening led to a cleansing, and cleansing prepared one for some further stage in a journey of the spirit.

Months later, in June, 1959, at another turning point, I picked up a book that had stood on our bookshelves in Jamaica, West Indies, unread since I had bought it two years earlier. It was a book that would change my life, for in it lay explained the interior evolution of the spirit. The author, Evelyn Underhill, called that evolution "the mystic way." Her book, published by E. P. Dutton, was called *Mysticism*.

Miss Underhill, who was born more than a hundred years ago in England, has been called the leading mystical theologian and writer on mysticism in our century. An Anglican, she was the first woman ever to be invited to lecture on religion at Oxford. She published more than thirty-five books, shedding light on the great mystics themselves as well as the mystical experience of God. She conducted retreats, lectured constantly, and wrote poetry, as well as producing her basic scholarly works. One or two are still big sellers in the spiritual field, in addition to the classic *Mysticism* which has gone through scores of printings since its publication in 1911. Every line she wrote has the vivid authenticity of one who has known for certain the love of God, as well as an ardent life of prayer to God. Yet all the while she was an active wife for her husband Hubert Stuart Moore, a London barrister. She was an expert yachtsman, a mountain climber, a constant traveler abroad. But her life was centered on God, union with Him, and union with human beings whom she constantly helped in their spiritual lives.

In *Mysticism*, her first major work on the subject, she tells us what the mystic way is, after defining mysticism:

> It is the name of that organic process which involves the perfect consummation of the love of God. . .it is the art of establishing. . .conscious relation with the Absolute.

The mystic way, or evolution of the life of the spirit, is built into each one of us. It is launched in us when and if we take the first step of awakening to the life of the spirit. Like biological evolution, the growth is upward. Unlike biology, it is not involuntary or inexorable. We must cooperate with the spirit, or the "Absolute" or "Reality," as Miss Underhill called God in this early work. I could accept her definition and her book because she did not seem to require that I believe in a personal god, Jesus Christ. In fact I learned later that Evelyn Underhill herself had written the book *Mysticism* more than ten years before she herself had a personal experience of Jesus as God.

But back in 1959, when I first read her book, I accepted the message she gave. *You are going somewhere* and that somewhere is up in a rising and dipping, but always mounting, journey to the goal of union with God. It is like a spiral stairway—two steps forward, one step back. This spiral evolution gives meaning to the seemingly disparate, unrelated incidents, accidents, sufferings, of your life, just as biological evolution gives order and meaning to life, from one cell up to a human being.

You are going somewhere. You are going on a journey toward uniting with God as you understand Him. If you don't want to call Him God, call it "Absolute," "Reality," "the One." This journey is begun by the One, guided by Him or it, and completed by

Him or it. But you do not have to believe God is a person in order to start the journey. You can believe, as I did, that there is something beyond yourself, a power greater than you. More than one million alcoholics are recovered from their dread disease because they came to believe in a God as they understand Him; anything larger than they—a group, the sky, the universe. So, if you are an unbeliever, just try today relying on some power, benign, of course, to launch your spiral journey.

Miss Underhill's book showed me that the survival kit is really the whole bag of tools, the set of instruments and equipment that you need for the spiral journey. The kit is the whole into which the parts, the tools, fit. And as I began to see the whole, my days and months and years began to reveal a pattern, a pattern of growth. Now I could and did begin to ". . .press toward the goal for the prize of the upward call. . ." (Philippians 3:14).

The goal beyond survival, that is, the goal of transcendence, has not only helped me to survive; it has led to a new way of life, one that encompasses both the events of each day and the tools. I have spent many years finding out about this survival kit. My wish is that I had found it earlier so that I could have started on my conscious journey of the spirit at an earlier age. But the good news is that, whatever age we are, we can start now building our own kit. And by using the tools in the kit we can become convergent people; that is, we can unite with God at the center, and with our neighbor at the circumference of life. As convergent people, each of us contributes to the great forward thrust of the planet itself, toward oneness, union with God. This converging of the spirit of all the people on our earth was first revealed to me by the works of the late Teilhard de Chardin, the French Jesuit and scientist-mystic.

Evelyn Underhill had taught me about the convergent person. Now Teilhard taught me about the convergent planet in his masterpiece, *The Phenomenon of Man* (Harper, 1959), and his other works. The English mystic taught me that I am going somewhere as a person. Teilhard said we are *all* going somewhere, all three billion fellow travelers on our spinning, fragile globe. We are all converging, that is, uniting, through communications, actions, thought, and spirit, orbiting in an upward spiral in our spaceship earth. And our orbit is not just around the sun; it is a spiraling upward orbit to God.

Now I began a search for a survival kit for the suffering planet, one that would oddly enough begin a synthesis of my own family heritage of working for the common good, the community, and my newer concern for the individual suffering human being.

I knew that we are already bound together, we sojourners in the spaceship earth, by our kinship of suffering, our kinship of survival. Teilhard urges that we transform that kinship, turn it into a kinship of dedication to promote the spiritual future of the human race, a converging humanity rising toward God. This kinship of dedication will not just happen as the result of evolution. It will only be brought about, says Teilhard, if humanity recognizes a transcendent, which alone can evoke universal love among men. That transcendent, he says, was incarnated as man in the person of Jesus Christ.

In later chapters, I will discuss some of the implications of converging humanity in a kinship of dedication For the first time in history we have the framework necessary for that convergence. We have a new breed of convergent persons, uniting in themselves concern for people and the planet; we have the revival and launching of convergent communities in small groups; and finally we have the unprecedented technology of the twentieth century which has already established convergence at the levels of communication and transportation. But, as with all change, we must start with the individual.

Survival kits for the individual as well as for the community run in my family. My late great-aunt, Susan B. Anthony, who won the vote for American women in the Nineteenth Amendment to the Constitution, ratified in 1920, herself formed a kit of tools to survive and ultimately transcend her fifty-five-year struggle for justice for blacks and women. Externally, her survival kit was a worn, battered, brown leather satchel. She toted it with her on the million-mile journeys she made campaigning to free all black people, and women, both black and white. The satchel contained her eye glasses, her tracts on abolition and suffrage, and copies of the legislation she tried to win to bring blacks and women equality under the law. The satchel also contained a beautiful red silk shawl that she wore over her sober black gowns when she spoke.

That red shawl, I believe, was the major tool in her survival kit. It was a living flame of love warming her on the cold platforms in dingy halls where audiences pelted her with rotten eggs, shouts, and abuse, or dozed in apathy. Of exquisite silk, with long heavy-knotted fringe, it was worn "with the grace of a Spanish belle," a reporter from the *Washington Star* said. When Aunt Susan was dressing for the huge thirtieth anniversary woman suffrage convention in Washington in 1898, one of her disciples persuaded her to substitute a new white shawl for the old red shawl. She appeared in the new one on the platform and was beginning her address. Suddenly a note was handed to her. Looking down her aquiline nose she read it, fearing bad news from home or from a new defeat in her cause. Instead she read:

No red shawl, no report.

Signed: The Press Table.

Then she read it aloud laughing, and said, "All right boys, I'll send to the hotel for it." When it arrived, she put it around her broad shoulders in a graceful way the reporter said was peculiarly her own. The audience broke into delighted applause. The reporters took up their pencils and began to write their stories.

That red shawl good-naturedly donned by Aunt Susan in the 1898 convention symbolizes why she survived all the disappointments, attacks, and failures of her long life. It was the banner of her crusade, a crusade born of love, not of impersonal social doctrine. That love was first for her father, Daniel Anthony, who reared her in the Quaker faith, a faith growing out of an in-dwelling spirit of love. That love focused not only on widespread suffering mankind, but on particular people: a panting fugitive slave at the station of the underground railroad, a woman unjustly convicted of murder. This widespread love to all in common extended to the poor, the blacks, the women who suffered. It also extended to their oppressors—the rich, the white, and the men.

Aunt Susan was a convergent person, united with

13

the spirit at her center and her neighbor at the circumference. Her red shawl was a mantle of her maternal orientation toward the world, an attitude that caused Gertrude Stein to name her "The Mother of Us All" in her opera written with Virgil Thompson. They show the real Aunt Susan in her compassion, but also with her major quality of hope, resilience, based on love.

I tried for years to follow in Aunt Susan's giant footsteps, as I related in *The Ghost in My Life*. Not only did I crusade against the injustice suffered by blacks and women, but against that suffered by the victims of war, fascism, and the poor. But the more I crusaded for the masses of humanity, the more alienated I seemed to become from individuals, including myself. I projected my unholy trinity of fear, frustration, and resentment on those I called the enemy, the oppressors. I was enveloped in no red shawl, no living flame of love, but rather hostility. Though my causes did good for others, I, as a person, was chilled and starving for lack of love. The symptom of that starvation was my disease of alcoholism, which stopped me in my mass crusading tracks at the age of thirty. My sister alcoholics on an "each-one-reach-one" basis rescued me and put me on the path of personal survival. Then I realized that I had reversed the process of growth. I had been trying to change the world before I had even begun to try to change myself. I bless my disease of alcoholism. It forced me to find my own survival kit. Today I carry that kit, not the worn brown satchel of Aunt Susan, but an invisible kit with tools given to me by her, my sister alcoholics, and a gallery of contemporaries, more precious to me than priceless portraits. Whenever I think I will not survive, let alone transcend the particular brand of suffering permitted in my spiral journey, I take out that gallery of supernatural courage, born of the love of God and the love of humanity.

This book is in part a gallery of these portraits, plus the tools the many have given me, and the tools given me by the One.

More important than their stories are the specific tools they give that will help you survive and transcend as you seek to fill your own survival kit. And equally vital is that you will be using these tools not only for yourself; you will be handing them on to your brothers and sisters all over the world so that they too may survive. And in doing this you can come to say, as Aunt Susan did despite all the setbacks and humiliations of her life, *"Failure is impossible."*

For, of course, failure *is* ultimately impossible, because *you are going somewhere*, not only as a solitary person, but as a solidary sojourner in the spaceship earth. You are going somewhere personally and collectively. You may describe that journey as a converging, rising one. Or you may use the language of religion and say, "Seek ye first the Kingdom of God, and His righteousness, and all these things shall be added unto you." Or you may use the language of the poet Gerard Manley Hopkins, who gives us a last and best reason for hope, hope for us personally, and hope for our planet, in his poem "God's Grandeur."

And though the last lights off the black West went
   Oh, morning, at the brown brink eastward,
   springs—

Survival Kit

Because the Holy Ghost over the bent
    World broods with warm breast and with ah!
    bright wings.

First Tools for Survival

1. You have survived to this moment. Be grateful.
2. To continue surviving you need at first only the flicker of a match worth of hope.
3. Nobody has a monopoly on suffering.
4. You are going somewhere.
5. "Failure is impossible." (Susan B. Anthony)

Chapter 2

Prayer: The Biggest Tool
in the Kit

Many of the tools in my survival kit I leave untouched for months at a time. I do not *remember to remember* to use them. Some I pick up only in major crises. But there is one tool without which I could not have survived at all. I have used it every day, many times a day, for many years, even when I did not see the sense of it. That is the master tool—prayer. It is the instrument that keeps all the other tools in working order.

I do not mean by prayer simply the "God help me" we all mutter in times of trouble. Nor do I mean the rote prayers that we have learned as children. I do not even mean the great liturgical prayers of the churches.

I mean by prayer the soul's spontaneous communication with God as we understand Him, vocal, silent, and, I would add, written.

It doesn't matter where or how you begin to pray. In fact you can begin to pray even if you don't really believe in God. If I had postponed talking and writing to God until I came to believe in Him, I would not have survived at all to become a believer. Prayer can actually build your faith; as a frantic father of an epileptic son said, ". . .Lord, I believe; help thou mine unbelief" (Mark 9:24).

One way to become a believer is to *pray as if you really do believe* someone is listening and that something is going to change. I began praying though

I didn't know I was, long before I had a conscious belief in anything. In *The Ghost in My Life*, I told the story of typing drunken scrawls on a yellow piece of paper at four o'clock in the morning. I was, in those days, telling the women of New York how to live right on daily radio, while I closed the bars of Greenwich Village each night. Those drunken words were:

"I am not really this bad—underneath this drunken, disgusting self, there is another self—someone who is not as bad as I am now."

Unorthodox as it was, this "prayer" led directly to my finding the men and women who rescued me and helped me to survive and stay sober. Two years later sobriety was just about the only positive credit I possessed. Everything else seemed out of joint. I was running up a huge debt supporting an expensive psychoanalysis that made me feel helpless. I was undergoing the unpleasant litigation of a traumatic divorce; and I had been blacklisted from my radio livelihood for my liberal crusades. I felt flattened out and scared as I walked one night to my lonely little Greenwhich Village apartment. It was then that a saving sentence, a preprayer tool floated into mind:

"Act as if you're cherished, loved, and secure."

I argued back, Who cherishes, loves me, or makes me secure? I am not first with anyone. I am insecure in all areas—no job, no husband, no true friend. But something impelled me to hang onto that sentence, to act as if indeed someone did cherish and love me, as if somehow I really were secure emotionally and financially. I practiced this not only when I was with people, I practiced it as I walked alone, sat in the subway, turned up the two flights of stairs to my walk-up. I held my head high, moved on the street, in a shop, or at home *as if* I were interiorly composed, *as if* some happy ending had already taken form.

I had been practicing this for only a month when an amazing thing happened. I woke in my apartment at the unusual (for me) hour of six o'clock, awakened to a burst of insight flooding me with new awareness. Suddenly in that early morning I felt one with everyone, with myself, truth, beauty, and goodness. Everything seemed heightened and everything seemed significant. I reached for my clipboard and scrawled out my certitude that life was love and love was life. I wrote and wrote, covering fifty pages before I got out of bed that morning. I felt light and clear and happy and free. I walked not on, but above the sidewalk, it seemed, as I went to the subway. I soared through the underground as though it were rocketing me from hell to paradise. I surfaced to look with love at greening Central Park and danced onto the bus that carried me eastward to my psychoanalyst. Eagerly I poured forth the insights of oneness, of truth, love, and of beauty that had risen to my conscious mind that morning. He termed them "free associations," a part of the analytic process. I wafted out of his office and on to the bus. I walked down Fifth Avenue in the afternoon which by now was darkened by clouds. But it was brilliant to me. The usually gray, blurred, anonymous faces of New Yorkers now seemed personalized, individualized, lightened in love.

This experience of "the golden and the singing" almost led me to the brink of an awakening. But out of ignorance and pigheadedness I did not grasp the further tools offered me. I survived the dubious excitement of that year, but only to succumb to situations that continued the cycle of suffering.

It was to survive another siege five years later when I grasped at the biggest tool in the kit. It came to me, *"Why not try prayer? You have tried everything else."*

I could not bring myself to pray out loud to the God in whom I did not believe. Instead I began to write to God on my clipboard, as though He did exist, and as though He did care for my problems. He answered, not with a dramatic flash but with a little lead showing that I was not so very far from shore, a lead I call a "land bird." That tiny answer was to place me on the very first stage of the journey of the life of the spirit. It gave me my first approach to an awakening to a higher power. And it had happened in my case through answered prayer. It can happen in other ways I was to learn when I read another book by Evelyn Underhill, *The Spiritual Life* (Harper, 1955). She put it this way:

> The moment in which, in one way or another, we become aware of this creative action of God and are therefore able to respond or resist, is the moment in which *our conscious spiritual life begins.* (Italics mine.)

From that moment of awakening onward I clutched the biggest tool in the kit, practiced it in writing, vocally, studied it, even helped write a book on it all within the next year. I did all of this despite the "cloud of unknowing" concealing the power I was praying to. And this proved to me that it does not really matter what your concept of God is in this first stage, awakening. The power can be the group helping you, even an impersonal power, an infinite, or life force, oversoul, absolute. The point is that once you have "become aware of this creative action of God" as you understand or do not understand Him, and begin talking, writing, and listening, you have taken hold of the tool of prayer, and your conscious spiritual life has begun.

When you are praying for sheer survival you do not quibble about theology. By admitting your dependence on anything larger than you, you are beginning to believe. But you must *remember to remember to pray*, not only in emergencies. Now you should start to practice some order in prayer, even if it is only five minutes you give a day, in addition to spot prayers throughout the day. Set a regular time for your exclusive attention to God, no matter how short; otherwise your first experience of the power of prayer may get lost in the distractions of daily life and you will slip back into the rut so common to most of us.

In my textbook on prayer, *The Prayer-Supported Apostle* (Catholic Action, 1965), I tell students that to find out what that rut is you simply analyze one day. You will learn that much of the time you and I are actually conducting a constant conversation with ourselves, about ourselves, our health, income tax problems, family feuds, or loneliness. These "monologues with me" are like scurrying little squirrels that run riot through your mind in the minutes in, say, a car, bus, or subway. The result is that you arrive at your destination with the problems further tangled and still unsolved because you have been limiting your consultation to the one who has the problem, the one who got you into it in the first place—yourself.

While you have been feeding your self-concern,

you have starved God out of your life. You cannot give your concern to two ideas at one time, you and the power. I cannot conduct a dialogue with God while I am immersed in a monologue with me. But if you remember to remember to *switch from a monologue with you to a dialogue with God*, you are not only handing over your problem to the power who has the solution, you are at the same time arousing your will to think about God and not your problem.

A friend of mine, Ruth, called me for comfort when she opened her mail and read a cold little note from her recently divorced husband. He did not want to hear from her ever again. He had just remarried. Ruth went into a state of shock, resentment, self-rejection, and the beginnings of a collapse. She was all set to let this news throw her back into hypochondria, visits to the doctor for shots, pills, even a nursing home. When we talked for an hour, she rehearsed every negative about her husband, her marriage, her future.

I listened; then I urged her to stop her monologue right now, and begin a dialogue with God, even if it only consisted of saying over and over again "God is with me." When I saw her late that night she had managed to try the switch. She had begun starving her own negative reactions, replacing them with a conversation with God in whom she does believe. Still later that night she put into practice another tool. She began to *free herself from the finite, by immersing herself in the infinite*. She was only able to do this for fifteen minutes, but she did it. She walked out underneath the stars, by the sea, and shed the blow to her pride, her worries, by dwelling for that brief time on the vastness of sea and sky and the soft tropical air.

Even you who live in crowded cities, as I have for long portions of my life, you can find some oasis of the infinite. When I was living in a cold midwestern city for four years, putting in a sixteen-hour day of study and a job, I finally found a park, a former bridle path through tall trees in a little frequented part of the forest. There I drove each day at the end of my five hours as student, and before starting my duties as dean for the next eight to ten hours. I parked the car and walked out into the woods, entered a pool of prayer as soon as my foot left the asphalt. There in that forest I was able to immerse in the infinite so that I could not only survive the long working day for four years, but actually came to enjoy it. I also proved that even South Bend, Indiana, can be beautiful in the midst of winter, if you are in a state of prayer and meditation.

Place is not important I learned back in Jamaica, West Indies, in the 1950s. My husband and I were entertaining a group of World War II veterans of the RAF Jamaica Squadron. They had flown out from England to the island for a commemorative visit. We had invited half a dozen of them for dinner. One of the men lingered with us, chatting and sipping the strong Jamaican coffee, while his friends roamed our farm, drinks in hand. This young man stood out from his friends by a certain maturity, even serenity. Now and then he threw in a Biblical phrase or verse. I was stunned that an RAF man on a lark in Jamaica would be so out of character. I asked him if he were a chaplain.

"No," he smiled, "but you nearly guessed it. I used to be a monk—an Anglican monk—at home in England. When war came, I felt I must serve in a more active way. I left and was promptly drafted by the RAF."

"But how could you bear it—how could you adjust," I asked, "to the dangerous, noisy, fragmented life of the RAF after your contemplative quiet of the monastery garden?"

He sat back in his chair, put his hands on the arms, "But isn't that the whole point, my dear? Isn't that the whole point of prayer that you should be able to get into the presence of God and stay there while repairing the wing of a plane—just as you do in the monastery garden?"

When I have complained that conditions interfere with my prayer life, I have remembered his words. And I have been able to train myself so that I can pray in a line at a supermarket, or in a doctor's crowded waiting room. But that is only after years of forming the habit of prayer. Our unruly minds prefer to drift in spotty, distracted worry while we are chauffeuring the children to school, riding a commuter train, or driving to work. Actually we can use those minutes, those hours, to worry about our suffering, or we can use them to pray. We have the choice. How do we *stop worrying and start praying?*

We start where we are; that is, we usually start praying for survival itself, survival from the particular brand of suffering, large or small, that has mowed us down today. Granted there are always those who have been given the grace of great faith, who move from strength to strength in the spirit throughout their lives. But most of us, as in my case, reach our spiritual awakening because our situation has forced us to ask:

"Why not try prayer? I have tried everything else."

And nine times out of ten, your first prayer will be the prayer of petition, that is, asking for help. You have been saying a kind of petition all of your life without knowing it. You have often said to yourself, "I wish that I could get over my fear," or you have muttered, "I hope that I will get through this exam," or "My dream is a life free of pain."

When you convert the wish, the hope, the dream, into a petition to the Power you may still not believe in, it becomes your first prayer. And though petition is the first stage of prayer, and the simplest, you will never abandon it entirely even after you have begun practicing meditation and have received the gift of contemplation. No matter how far we go in the life of the spirit, we can still be brought low by our body-soul composite. And it is for our bodies that we often make our first petition for help. The great teacher has repeatedly instructed us to pray not only for our spiritual, emotional needs, but for our daily bread, our healing, our life itself.

Another prayer teacher, that sinner turned saint, Augustine, wrote authoritatively centuries ago, "It is proper to pray for what it is proper to desire." That means "things," not only graces from God. It also means little things as well as big things. So whatever it is reasonable, lawful, proper to desire, it is reasonable, lawful, and proper to pray for. That is a first rule on the prayer of petition. Later I shall mention some of the conditions modifying the rule. Right now it is safe to say that we should pray in boldness, claiming what it is proper to desire. And it is certainly proper to desire to be alive and well and free of suffering.

One of my long-time friends, we'll call her Dorrie,

a working wife, was given the dread diagnosis of cancer of the uterus. As she walked out of the doctor's office, she caught herself succumbing to the panic caused by that word, cancer, and that disease. But having spent years in prayer and in prayer groups, she forced herself to do what she had told others to do. She called her prayer partner, a member of her own church. She flatly told her the news and asked her to pray and to notify other prayer groups, if she would, of the date of surgery. She asked that they pray for a complete healing of cancer, and a quick recovery from the hysterectomy and cobalt treatments. She also placed a call to me. I, in turn, mobilized our Florida prayer groups.

Five months after the surgery, Dorrie, her husband and I attended a cocktail-dinner party in her city. She had already that day spent not only her usual long hours at work, but had taken a swim with me before the party. Now I marveled at her frankness. Friends who had not seen her since the surgery carefully asked her how she was.

"I'm fine," she said with her vivid smile. "I *did* have cancer. But now I am all better. Thank you for your prayers."

Many more than five years have passed since then. She has, through prayer, been able to keep her mind clear of the usual fear of cancer patients that there will be a recurrence. She continues to ask for prayers especially when she has her periodic check-ups. So far—and the fateful five years have long since passed—she has never lost a day's work since the original surgery, never had the slightest trace of malignancy. Dorrie likes to quote from a prayer of mine, "The more perfect my confidence in Thee,/The more special Thy Providence to me."

Martha, another friend, came home from the market one afternoon to find that her fifteen-year-old had vanished. She learned later, from a schoolmate of his, that her son Bobby had run away from home. She called me and the prayer community to join in a prayer watch for Bobby's safe and immediate return. We prayed first of all for Martha, to dissolve her fear, to stop her speculation about where he might be, what might happen to him.

After a long weekend, Bobby called. He had "run away" to his big brother's college in the Midwest. He had done it all, he said proudly, on two dollars, hitch-hiking, sleeping in fields. He was coming home tomorrow. Though Martha rejoiced that he was safe, she asked us to pray on how to deal with his absence without leave. The answer was firmness, a change of schools, and more communication between his father and him. He then went back to school, a different one. He even joined his own informal kind of prayer group with other teen-agers in a church production of *Jesus Christ Superstar*. Some time later he asked me for a cross to wear on his leather thong necklace.

Dorrie's and Martha's prayers were for concrete specific healings of body and situation. They did not try to pray alone. They called on the prayer groups nearest them for prayer support and for ventilating their suffering. In so doing they helped us who prayed for them as well as receiving their own healings. We ourselves had a vacation from ourselves while praying for our friends. We put our own sufferings on ice, gave them a chance to cool, gave our prayers for ourselves a chance to work. This is extremely effective in preventing you from diluting your prayer through fear and doubt. When you are interceding for someone else, you do not have time to watch nervously for the results of your personal petitions. You give your answer time to bud, then flower. I call this: *Heal others to heal yourself.*

I went to one group in our South Florida prayer community one night, worried about a sore tongue. A jagged crown of a tooth had cut it and it had not healed. Though the doctor insisted it was not precancerous, I had formed the habit of running my tongue over the rough tooth making it worse. I asked the group to pray for medical or dental help on this nagging irritation, or even a direct healing from God.

At the same meeting, Tom, who owned a small business of electrical appliances, opened up for the first time to the fact that he was suffering from glaucoma, and that it was getting worse. In fact, his doctor had warned him that unless the strong new eye drops radically halted the deterioration, he faced surgery that might lead to cataracts in his case. He told us he had not asked us to pray before because he felt his deafness was the greater problem. But now he was desperate. If his eyes went, he would no longer be able to read lips to help his understanding.

We laid hands on him that night in prayer. Two days later, he said he was not a bit better. He was sure his doctor would insist on surgery. I prayed for him again and urged him to skip work the next morning and attend a prayer group meeting at eleven A.M. He said he couldn't, he had too much work at the shop. In my prayers the following day it came to me strongly that he must attend the meeting, that he would be healed if he put himself out to go the uttermost mile. He stalled when I called him. Then I insisted, as his prayer teacher, that he really must go, and I offered to drive him there. He finally agreed to go, to drive himself. I carried him in intercession all day while writing, totally forgetting to worry my tongue over my rough tooth.

That night Tom called, saying, "They gave the whole prayer meeting over to praying for my eyes. I opened up as I never have before. Then I went right to the eye appointment."

The doctor tested one eye and said that he couldn't understand what had happened, but not to get his hopes up before he examined Tom's other eye. Then he put down his instruments and, looking baffled at what he called a "miraculous" improvement, asked, "What happened? You're so much better I don't even want to see you again for six months."

Tom told him that his eye drops could only claim part of the credit. The rest belonged to God. We knew that the healing belonged to the Lord in any case. As for me, I was so exalted and refreshed by his good news and the vacation which I had given my own suffering that I was ready for my own healing. It took place a few days later. *Heal others to heal yourself* had worked once more. Not that I had done any healing, but I had gotten myself out of the way to become one channel for God to heal Tom while allowing Him to heal me.

You'd expect a priest to pray. But not all priests combine prayer with using their wit and their wits to save themselves from death. The Reverend Louis J. Putz, C.S.C., of Notre Dame, Indiana, my spiritual director since 1961, used all three back in 1939 when he was trapped in France at the outbreak of war.

German-born, Father Putz ran away from home to

the United States when he was only fourteen years old. His aunt, a nun living in this country, promptly put him in Moreau Seminary, the one he would later direct at the University of Notre Dame in South Bend. He was ordained a priest of the Congregation of the Holy Cross, founded at Le Mans, France. After ordination, he returned to Paris for further study while serving as one of that band of convergent people, the "worker-priests," men who carried the gospel into the factories and slums of France, living and working like the poor they served. He was in Paris when World War II broke out in September, 1939. He was caught in the precarious situation of being a German national complete with Hitler's swastika on his passport.

Realizing that his only hope for survival lay in getting to America, he went straight to the American embassy, hoping he could get a visa. Of course it was Saturday; the embassy was closed to business. But Father persisted until he found a vice-consul to hear him.

"But how do I know that you have a job awaiting you in the United States?" the consul asked suspiciously. "Why should I believe that this cable you show me was sent from there? You could send yourself this cable!"

Father Putz stood in silent prayer while his life depended on this man's believing him. The vice-consul decided to test him.

"Okay, Father, prove to me that you know South Bend. What shirt factory is located there?"

"Wilson," said Father Putz promptly. "I'm even wearing a Wilson shirt. Here, look at my label."

Prayer and quick wits had won the first round. The consul granted him the visa. Triumphantly, Father

Putz stepped outside the embassy with his precious visa in hand. He was stopped on the steps by French police. He was arrested and herded with other aliens to a make-shift concentration camp—the largest stadium in Paris, the Bois de Colombes.

Again he prayed for one thing: to get out of this place, for he knew that this would be just the embarkation point for deportation to a Nazi death camp. He was guided in prayer to ask the impossible—permission to leave the camp, go out and cross the street to a church and obtain vessels for celebrating Mass in the prison camp. Miraculously his jailers granted him that permission. That was the last they ever saw of Father. He kept right on going from the church to Le Mans, headquarters of his monastic order. There he was placed under house arrest for two months. He spent those two months not fretting, but planning. He knew that his German relatives' anti-Nazi opinions and actions would mean death if he were deported. He knew he must go to the one place in the world that offered him a chance to live and work for the Lord: Notre Dame, Indiana. He prayed, yes, but he also followed the teaching of St. Augustine:

> *Pray as if everything depends on God: act as if everything depends on you.* (Italics mine.)

Keeping his wits about him, he found out that a ship was sailing for the United States. But how could he possibly get on board? He had no ticket, no exit visa necessary to leave wartime France. But he did have a priceless letter of safe conduct. Earlier, before the war, he had been confessor to a French general.

The latter had given him a letter "To Whom It May Concern" asking that the bearer, Father Louis Putz, be granted safe conduct in France. Armed with this and further prayer, Father Putz managed to get onto a troop train, on Novemeber 11, 1939, a train leaving for Le Havre and his hoped-for passage. During an air raid, everyone had to disembark and seek shelter. Finally at Le Havre he muttered Hail Mary's all the way to the port in the taxi, a ride of five miles. He found refuge that night at a convent where the sisters joined him in prayer for his hoped-for voyage. Boldly he showed the general's letter to the British Tommies guarding the port next morning. One glance at the signature, and they actually saluted him on board.

He spent most of the crossing to England offering up prayers of thanksgiving. But they were premature. He was ordered to try a French ship as the only chance to sail to America. He tried to book a ticket only to learn that the franc had fallen, leaving him short of the necessary money for his passage. He made another try on another day at the French shipping line. The franc had by odd coincidence rallied that day, enough to pay for his ticket, and give him a tiny bit of change.

The voyage itself was a dangerous one. Daily ditching drills were ordered by ship's officers. They knew that they were surrounded by Nazi submarines infesting the waters, plus a giant German battleship, the *Bismarck*, prowling in the area.

"I really learned to pray during those risky days," Father said. "I also learned total resignation to God's will. I was surrendered."

But they made it to Ellis Island, New York. Now the French wanted to bar him from landing. They suspected he was a Nazi spy cloaked in clerical robes as a cover. While they sent all the other passengers, mostly Jewish refugees from Hitler, to line up alphabetically, they ordered Father Putz brusquely to the end of the line.

"I was fortunate that I had found a friend to stand with me, a friend I first found in the Gospels back on another voyage in 1923. That was my first real contact with Christ."

Now in 1939, Father clutched the hand of his invisible friend, praying that He would find a way to let him enter the only country in which he could stay alive and serve Him. American immigration officials interrupted his praying. The French guards, assuming that the Americans were on to this impostor, pushed Father roughly forward to them. Father stood before the interrogators, begging Jesus for the best, but prepared for the worst.

Suddenly an American voice boomed out, "How come Iowa smeared the Irish last week?" An officer was asking Father this with a grin. "I lost money on the game."

Stunned, and then breaking into a big smile, Father could only stare for a moment. The immigration doctor was a graduate of Notre Dame. He had recognized Father. Suddenly the suspected Nazi spy became almost a hero. The French guards apologized profusely. Father was ushered through customs like a VIP. He then made his way to Grand Central Station. His next need was a ticket to South Bend. But his money would not cover the full fare.

Silent prayer and his wits again came to the rescue. Quickly and authoritatively he asked for the clergyman's travel discount. The clerk asked him, in turn, if he was registered in the directory of American priests who were eligible for such discounts. Asking the Lord's forgiveness, Father told a lie. He said, yes, he was registered, knowing full well he could not possibly be listed. After all, he was a German priest who had been serving in France. He waited while the clerk pulled out the priests' directory. The clerk finally looked up, saying:

"Why, yes, you're right here—the Reverend Louis Putz, Iowa."

Father could scarcely believe his ears. But it was so. There was a Father Putz, and his clerical discount enabled my Father Putz to board the train for Notre Dame, where he has served ever since in many professional capacities. In more recent years he founded and became president of Fides Publishers, and until 1971 was rector of Moreau Seminary. His gratitude for his escape from death in a Nazi camp and his survival has been shown in the help he has poured out to others, individually and in groups, especially lay persons, which is how I met him.

Father Putz survived by using the biggest tool in the kit—prayer. He also helped thousands of others survive by prayer when he helped me launch the spontaneous prayer group movement in the Church at Saint Mary's, Notre Dame, back in 1965. This breakthrough later germinated and proliferated in the 1970s prayer group movement, reaching more than one million lay persons, priests, and nuns.

We will talk more about prayer groups in later chapters. Right now the point is to get started in your own prayer life. Start with whatever problem is uppermost in your mind, physical, mental, spiritual, or even material.

Some people think it is wrong to "use" prayer to accomplish material gain in our lives. Again St. Augustine clears up the theological issue, saying, *"It is proper to pray for what it is proper to desire."* (Italics mine).

Two of the most saintly people I have ever met in my life demonstrated not only the propriety, but even the holiness, of praying for such "worldly" things as food on the table, shoes for the children, money to buy gas for the car. They were the late Reverend Francis and Jessie Cook. Francis told me about this when I first met him years ago:

"We prefer soup bones with children to T-bones alone."

The Cooks learned when they were first married that they could not give birth to their own children. Francis, a Methodist minister in the Appalachian mountains of Kentucky was fifty-three, and Jessie thirty-eight, when they adopted their first children, beginning a ministry to and for children that would lead to the legal adoption of nine boys and girls, plus educating sixty foreign students.

The Cooks were able not only to survive but to transcend their poverty while rearing their children and educating the foreign young. They did it by prayer, according to their own words. Neither poverty, nor their ages, nor the ages of the children stopped the ministry to children launched by the Cooks in 1929. Jessie said to me when I spent five days with them at their simple little house in Vista, California:

My only interest in telling our story is that others in humble walks of life shall be encouraged to adopt children and joyously expend

35

themselves on behalf of others less fortunate than themselves.

With no salary, and only a run-down farm that they had acquired with some money inherited by Jessie, the couple worked from dawn till midnight supporting their growing brood. The Cooks adopted children who were all over two years old, save one. They proved that love and prayer, not income or youth, are the chief factors in successfully rearing and educating children. In 1949 they auctioned off the farm. Francis went to work at the age of seventy-five as a janitor-guard at Camp Pendleton, California. He got up at 3:45 A.M. daily to drive more than an hour with Jessie, who worked as mess attendant at the camp hospital. A heart attack stopped Jessie's job at the hospital. But it did not stop her cooking, cleaning, and washing for her children.

"Every mother, mother another" was her way of setting her goal for herself and other women.

She and Francis had begun with a dream and moved on to its realization through prayer and hard work. A descendant of John and Priscilla Alden, Francis met his Jessie, herself descended from the Pilgrims, at the Boston University School of Theology. After three years of marriage that produced no children of their own, they began to pray for children to adopt. It wasn't all that easy. There were just no children to adopt in New Hampshire, where Jessie had journeyed to find them. When she was about to give up hope of ever finding a baby, she sought comfort from her father, the president of Colby College, and executive secretary of the American Baptist Home Mission Society.

He and she knelt in prayer at his home. He assured her afterward: "You will come back with a baby in your arms." Three months and hundreds of miles later, she found not a baby, but a five-year-old boy. When she wrote Francis, he said: "We're not going to leave the little sister behind." So they also took the chubby four-year-old redhead. Jessie journeyed with the two strange children from New Hampshire to Kentucky by car, train, ferry, and bus. Francis greeted his new family at their home in a way Jessie never forgot. "In front of a roaring fire was a little chair with a big doll in it—and on the other side of the fire, a toy drum. The house was a bower of flowers."

That was the beginning of their ministry to children. Nor did they limit themselves to Americans. They went on to sponsor teen-age Indonesian, Arab, Hungarian, and American Indian students, and even some grown-ups. Their home became "a house of prayer for all nations," as the prophet Isaiah had said centuries before Christ. And a large part of that prayer was for food, clothing, and education necessary for their children.

Whenever I hear someone object to asking God for "things" as well as spiritual progress, I tell them the story of Francis and Jessie Cook. They prayed for material goods, not for accumulating wealth, but for what it was proper to desire, the means of living for their growing family. They also practiced, *"When you pray for potatoes, reach for a hoe"* (italics mine), a saying of a Catholic priest, simplifying St. Augustine's statement on prayer. They worked long and hard with their hands to support that family.

The Cooks did not limit their prayers to asking becoming things of God. They practiced ceaseless thanksgiving and praise; in fact, they conducted a constant conversation with God twenty-four hours a day. They also practiced the other side of the life of prayer, cleansing and detachment. They disciplined and denied themselves in order to give to their children. I will never forget how I felt when Francis said to me gently as I sat rocking with him on the verandah of their bungalow, smoking a cigarette, "Do you realize, Susan, that four cartons of cigarettes a month would feed a starving child—very well—in Asia?"

However, even then I did not stop smoking until thirteen years later in 1973.

Tools for Waking Up to the Power of Prayer

1. Act as if you're cherished, loved and secure.
2. Try putting your prayers on paper.
3. Switch from a monologue with yourself to a dialogue with God.
4. Remember to remember to pray.
5. Free yourself from the finite by immersing yourself in the infinite.
6. Why not try prayer? You have tried everything else.
7. Stop worrying and start praying.
8. "It is proper to pray for what it is proper to desire." (St. Augustine)
9. Heal others to heal yourself.
10. "The more perfect my confidence in Thee, The more special Thy Providence to me." (Author's poem)
11. "Pray as if everything depends on God; act as if everything depends on you." (St. Augustine)
12. "When you pray for potatoes, reach for a hoe." (Father Pfau)

Chapter 3

There'll Always be a Barracuda

One day I was snorkeling in my beloved subtropical sea, gazing through my glass mask at the waving sea fans, white coral, and multicolored parrot fish. I felt one with the whole underwater world, praising God in His creation, and His creation in God.

Pollywogging, that is, undulating my body so that I wouldn't splash and disturb the fish, I was moving gently toward the reef and its greater beauties. I glided through the water happily lightened by my flippers. Suddenly, swiftly, a gray submarine-shaped fish streaked into view, his perpetual sneer broken by a snapping motion that revealed his razor-sharp teeth. Barracuda!

As I had been trained to do, I kept my eyes on him while I treaded water, stretching out so he would see that I was a far bigger fish then he, not just a hand or foot that he would like for dinner. He remained hovering, looking at me. Carefully, carefully, without splashing, I kept my eyes on him while I backed away with a special stroke I had learned for such perilous occasions. He took another glare at me, then swished about-face and streaked away out of sight. Since I was alone, I did not continue out to the reef, but swam back to shore, fretting that he had ruined the brilliance of my underwater hours. I asked:

"Will there always be a barracuda?"

Will there always be something to bar my

breakthrough to joy, something that shatters the calm? For I realized as I neared the shore that barracudas lurk not just in southern seas, but wait for all of us on the beach. They are the hurts and defects that hover ready to mar our day, our lives. They are the forms of suffering ready to strike with razor teeth.

You can't ignore barracuda either barring your way to the ocean reef, or the real-life barracuda that bar your *breakthrough from what you are to what God wants you to be*. Once you have reached the first stage of awakening to the goal beyond sheer survival, the goal of transcendence, you must take the initiative in coping with barracuda.

If you don't take the initiative you may not even survive. The hurts, the defects, the suffering, require, even demand, that *you act*. And that action is called stripping and cleansing. You are given plenty of tools for this stage of the journey of the life of the spirit. But *if you do not act to use these tools, they boomerang and hurt you*. Awakening and the prayer of petition have begun your journey from survival to transcendence. Now you must begin to pick up the sharp tools given you to strip and cleanse the old self. As Evelyn Underhill says, ". . .The spiritual life involves both *dealing with ourselves* and *attending to God*. . ."

Attending to God refers to our prayer and life toward God. Dealing with ourselves means ". . .killing the very roots of self-love: pride and possessiveness, anger and violence, ambition and greed, in all their disguises however respectable those disguises may be, whatever uniforms they wear. In fact, it really means the entire transformation of our personal, professional and political life. . ." (*The*

Spiritual Life, Harper, 1955).

Dealing with ourselves was called, by the traditional spiritual writers, mortification and detachment. The mortification or cleansing process means for us a ruthless cutting out of some of the basic causes of our suffering, our defects, using the astringents of stripping and cleansing. Detachment means not being run by any of our three major drives—for material goods, for sexual gratification, or for triumph of our own will.

For it is the old self, the self full of pride and possessiveness, of anger and violence, ambition and greed, that mars the moment or the month. These defects are like the barracuda hovering to snap at you and even to tear you apart.

The old self was described by St. Paul when he said:

For I do not do what I want, but I do the very thing I hate. (Romans 7:15)

Your old self, if you observe it even for a day, suffers a sense of unease, of being divided, of having your hands tied behind your back. A shadow is seen, falling between your bright aspirations and your impotence to carry them out. The moment you start the spiritual awakening process that unease festers like wounds received from a sea porcupine. The poisoned quills can infect unless you take a knife and cut them out.

You could get away with some of your defects before you awakened to the need for more than survival of suffering. Then you were able to indulge in a temper, arrogance, gossip, even lying. Now, however, your new awareness makes you vulnerable to those fevered eruptions. Now you are told by that inner voice: *"If you don't take the initiative, it will take you."*

If you don't start stripping and cleansing the old self right now, you will be handed some involuntary suffering even worse than your original plight. One reason for this is that now you know better. Before, you suffered in ignorance. Now you aspire to the new self, and that new self meets head on with the habit patterns of the old self. You have in fact entered what is called the purgative stage of the life of the spirit. Here you get an acute consciousness of the need to change if you are to survive at all. The tools you are given are active and voluntary ones that will help you start to shave, pare, trim, root out the defects that are hampering your efforts to survive and to transcend. By using these tools voluntarily, you'll feel a sense of achievement, or rigor, of asceticism—the same kind experienced by an athlete training for a game; a musician practicing for a concert. It involves a self-denial, a custody of the heart, a watching and correcting, that is made not just bearable, but challenging because of the high goal sought.

Do not deplore your defect and the suffering it causes. Consider it instead a "happy hurt." I came to see even my alcoholism as a "happy hurt," for without it I would not have found the tools of the survival kit; without it, I might not have found God. And it is certain that I would never have begun the stripping and cleansing process when I did. I did not seek purgation. It was forced upon me for sheer physical survival. I did not choose to strip myself of drink; it was a matter of life or death.

My "happy hurt" of alcoholism and its train of defects gave me my novitiate in the practice of mortification and detachment. *I did not try to go it alone.* My first kinship of suffering with recovering alcoholics helped me by giving me the tools to stay sober and to clean up the rest of my life. I used help and the tools to stay sober, but I did not go on and clean up the rest of my life. Despite others' warnings that I must ensure my sobriety by transforming the old self into a new self, I ignored their suggestions.

Instead, I grabbed only the tool of the prayer of petition, demanding from God everything from a new apartment to a new husband. And when the new husband appeared, as if he were an answer to my prayer, he and I moved to his home island of Jamaica to a hillside plantation. Then I doubled my demands on God, praying for a baby, for my husband's success, for prosperity. Instead of these boons I got a huge overdraft in the bank, trials by fire, flood, wreck, and violence. I got not bread but a stone.

Only then did I recall the forty days and nights of Jesus in the wilderness, the purging he endured. And I remembered Dante's *Purgatorio*, and the words "purgatory," "purging," "purgation," "cleansing," "purification," as I wrote later in an essay published in a book *As the Spirit Leads Us* (edited by Kevin and Dorothy Ranaghan, Paulist Press, 1971). These words did come to me, forcing me to ask myself, Was it possible that these trials I had undergone showed that I, Susan, needed a cleansing, a mortification, a purification? But my mind recoiled from those words. What more could I possibly need than sobriety, spiritual awakening, and the practice of the prayer of petition?

But the truth was that I did need something more in order to survive the ordeals I had suffered. I did need to look within, to throw out the old, stale ideas that had festered, fed on me, and all but destroyed me. I did need to strip myself of bondage to the devil of dubious excitement that had kept me in a frenetic, motor-minded state of activity for years, not just as reporter of crises, but as a survivor and magnet of crises. It was as though I attracted these fires, floods, wrecks, disasters into my orbit. And there was another bondage, another devil, the devil of compulsive desire, "I want what I want when I want it."

Perhaps since I had failed to take the initiative in cleansing, God had permitted these trials and ordeals to knock me flat as I was at that moment, flat out with flu. Even as I lay there, I knew that this was a decisive insight, a goad prodding me to undertake *voluntary* cleansing and stripping of the defects I had allowed to remain intact. Still I tarried. Again the action was taken out of my hands. I was amputated from my marriage in a nightmare of intolerable tension, duplicity, and threats against my life. The day after my husband forced me out of our home to make way for his new love, I was numbed with shock. Then it was another man, instantly appeared, inviting me to blot out my rejection through an affair with him. At this point I heard my quick reply without knowing I was saying it:

"If that's all I have learned to do these many years—then I might as well slit my throat."

And that strange sentence, refusing a rebound affair, though I did not realize it, began the stripping of my life-long pattern with men—out of the frying pan into the fire, out with the old, in with the new. Until that sentence came out of me, the mere thought of a month without male companionship had been inconceivable. Later, another strange sentence came to me:

"Why not—just for one year—give to God the time, energy, and attention you have given to men for the last twenty-five years?"

My answer till then to most of my suffering had been to submerge it in a passionate love affair. I had used some of my men purely as escapes from my problems. I had been, I realized, almost as compulsive about the ceaseless stream of men in my life as I had been about the booze in my life before I sobered up.

Now I took up the tools that had helped me strip down from alcoholism. I practiced those methods that I had used to stay away from a drink, to stay away from a compulsive rebound affair. I said and practiced:

"Just for today, this day only, I will not fall into bed with a man out of loneliness or spite or rebound."

But the old habit of a man-centered life was hard to break. The very first unmarried man I met after I left Jamaica proved nearly irresistible. I found myself on the brink of running off to Mexico for a quick divorce so that I could marry him. I had, in fact, just completed plans for this precipitous flight into a new marriage when I came to a full stop. I was stopped while sitting on a bus en route to meet him. I was stopped by the sense of a hand on mine, warning me, "Don't go."

Even though I didn't heed that warning immediately, I found myself in a week on a plane headed thousands of miles away from the tempting man. Later I learned we would have been exactly wrong for each other. Not only was he fast approaching alcoholism, but he had been sleeping with another woman all the time he had been supposedly courting me! That should have helped me keep to my vow for the year. But it did not.

A few months later I was about to settle on a lanky artist who also appealed to my maternal instinct because of his tales of woe. *Now I knew I couldn't resist alone, couldn't go it alone. I needed the help of others, other human beings. I needed a fellowship to help me.* I had long since used up any will power I had. Now I had to admit my powerlessness and really ask a higher power to help me.

Thus it was that, to help myself survive without a new man, I founded my first breakthrough prayer-share group. I called it that because I knew I must make a breakthrough from what I was to what I wanted to be. I started with my own defect that cried for change, my compulsion to start a new affair. A dozen men and women miraculously appeared who also wanted to make a breakthrough on our common problem of compulsive, impulsive involvements with the other sex. We called it "Mismated Anonymous," following the pattern of the Twelve Steps of Alcoholics Anonymous—steps that are actually the classical stages of the life of the spirit that Evelyn Underhill had taught me.

The steps in the life of the spirit embody the stages from awakening, prayer, cleansing, illumination, the dark night of the soul, and surrender, to the goal of union with God. They begin when you admit your own human powerlessness, as we did over our compulsive emotions. They are based on a belief in a higher power. They are only effective if you carry the message to others suffering as you are.

Each of us in the group was helped. One glamorous young mother was on the verge of making a third wrong marriage. One young man had never had any successful relationship with a girl. He was compelled, he learned in the group, simply compelled, to fail. At last he began to see why in our group discussions. He saw that he was so self-rejecting that he had to seek rejections from others. Of course he got them. A married woman was about to divorce her husband because of all his faults. She began in the group to see where *she* just might possibly be lacking in perfection. Her husband joined her at the meetings and together they started to work out their problems.

The help the others got at the weekly breakthrough meetings was nothing compared to the help I got from working with them. Not only was I on call, as they were, to aid the other is staying away from a slip into the compulsive pattern, but I was protected from a new mistake. The group carried me through those difficult, lonely months without my husband, and without the life-long expected new man.

That first breakthrough group, back in 1960, of Mismated Anonymous helped me to adapt AA's Twelve Steps to "The Seven Steps of Breakthrough" which I list at the end of this chapter. It also gave me the pattern for prayer-share groups which led to the national prayer-share movement we launched a few years later at Notre Dame, Indiana. It led further to the first national spontaneous prayer conference in the Catholic church, and to the first national ecumenical prayer conference among Roman Catholics and non-Catholics.

A further result was that the prayer-share groups'

practice of spontaneous prayer led to a breakthrough from rote prayer in the Roman church, laying the groundwork for the charismatic renewal with one million and more Roman Catholics praying as freely as their Protestant brothers.

The first breakthrough group, Mismated Anonymous, showed me that *each one reach one* applies to any "happy hurt," not just to alcoholism. It also applies to cleansing or stripping interior problems as well as exterior acts.

Through the group I saw once more that *you are helped where you hurt*, that your suffering can be transformed into a "happy hurt" the moment you *share in a fellowship of depth with others who are growing in the spirit. Don't try to go it alone. Choose the major defect that is hampering you and let it go one day at a time.*

Practice *custody of the heart*; that is, watch what your defect is doing; be aware of it. I also learned that working on one particular defect helps you *kick the pattern of problem addiction*. While you are ridding yourself of one barracuda, you begin to see the school of barracuda in the distance. In other words, you start cleansing the old self that wants to generate a whole school of new problems to substitute for the one defect you are getting rid of. You learn the meaning of the Lord's words:

When the unclean spirit has gone out of a man, he passes through waterless places seeking rest, but he finds none. Then he says, "I will return to my house from which I came." And when he comes he finds it empty, swept, and put in order. Then he goes and brings with him seven other spirits more evil than himself, and they enter and dwell there; and the last state of that man becomes worse than the first. (Matthew 12:43-45)

The defect-creating machine is the old self. There is no way except transformation of that self to rid ourselves of the bulk of our defects. And supernature abhors a vacuum just as does nature. In other words, the time, energy, and attention that once went into the habit of alcoholism, compulsive sex, gossip, lying, greed, or bitterness must be transmuted actively to new channels. Otherwise "the last state of that man becomes worse than the first."

Some defects stem, however, from life experiences that we did nothing to bring about. Sarah Gainham waged a lifelong battle against the bitterness imbedded in her heart. And if anyone ever had a cause to be bitter, Sarah had. Sarah, as a little girl in the West of the 1920s, worshipped one person in the world, her father. She loved her mother, but, as she says:

Dad was my life—and I am just so sure that this wonderful love I had for my first four years has made it possible for me when I got through my difficult years to be able to receive love and be able to give love. If I had had an unhappy beginning, I really don't know what might have happened to me. But I do have this base that I can go back to.

Sarah had just turned four in August, 1922. Her dad ran a store and post office near the border of Mexico in a little mining town in New Mexico up in the mountains. The Gainhams were the only

"Anglos" in town. They were surrounded by Mexicans in the mine, the houses, and the huts. They themselves lived over the store and post office. Her dad was a very brave man. He took over the store despite the fact that the two men who had kept it before him had just been murdered. "My dad went in and cleaned up the blood from their bodies and moved us in. He was so trusting, so sure that God just couldn't let anything happen to his family that he knew we would be all right."

On a day in August, Sarah's two aunts were both visiting, young ladies of sixteen and twenty-four. Sarah was the only child living with the four adults. That day her mother and she were upstairs. Sarah remembers the exact moment of the tragedy. She was at the kitchen sink, standing on a chair while her mother helped her get a drink of water.

Suddenly there was a strange and loud noise, a kind of commotion. Her mother ran to the stairway that went down to the store. Sarah heard her calling her father, "Bill! Bill!"

Her mother went down the stairs. She never came back. Little Sarah ran to see what had happened down there. It just seemed like blackness and noise to the child—nothing registered. She turned and ran onto the big second-story screened porch. One of the seven killers involved chased the four-year-old child.

"I can still hear his spurs and his chaps—knowing he was right behind me. Then I fell—flat on my stomach. I'll never know why he turned around and left me alive."

The sixteen-year-old aunt picked her up and rushed her to a little bunkhouse on the property. They cowered there while shouts and shots rang out against the hillside. The older aunt was still upstairs in the house. Later she told Sarah what had happened in that house.

One of the men stood at arm's length from the young woman. He shot her directly—aiming at her forehead. At that same instant she had thrown up her hands to her head. The bullet, instead of crashing through her brain, went up and skimmed the outside of her hand across the knuckles. She fainted at the shot. The murderer, seeing the blood, thought it was from her head and left her for dead. When she came to from her faint, she saw beside her the bullet riddled bloody bodies of Sarah's mother and father. She ran out to the bunkhouse where she hid with Sarah and the younger aunt until two trappers who lived there finally came home. Only then did Sarah hear the full story as her aunt poured it out to the trappers. Both of her parents had been shot to death. The aunts took Sarah back to the house, trying to keep the little girl from seeing the corpses of her beloved dad and her mother.

"I never saw them again."

The seven murderers had been hired by another Anglo to kill her father, she learned later. The cause? He would not sell liquor in the store. The murderer wanted to turn it into a saloon, to make money by selling booze to the poverty-stricken Mexicans.

As he lay dying, her father had tried to save his family. They found the circle of bullets he had made as he emptied his gun on the door.

"They killed my mother and took their rifle butts to bash out her teeth because of the gold fillings."

The shock blacked out the little girl's memory of the day of the murder and the funeral and even the trip east to Texas with her older aunt, the only relative left to care for her. As Sarah said later, "I don't remember much except the almost physical yearning for my dad and mother. I never cried in front of anyone, but I sobbed my heart out when I was alone."

The murder of her parents and her own near-murder were just the beginning of a long dark night in her life. Her older aunt adopted her, moved to New Mexico, and married. Now in Sarah's clouded vision she was torn between fear of her new stepfather, who claimed the aunt's time, and resentment that her own beloved parents had been killed, Sarah understandably became a behavior problem. She lay on the floor and screamed in temper tantrums. She begged her aunt not to leave her. Her aunt threatened her with punishments, which only made Sarah worse. She could not begin to love her stepfather, who could not understand children. But she later found two father images: one, a high school principal, the other, another older man on a summer vacation. These two men became the substitutes on whom she poured the love she had held for her dad. They helped her survive the dark years that lasted not only until her marriage at the age of nineteen, but even through her own motherhood of two children. No spiritual guide appeared to warn her that she must rid herself of her bitterness toward her aunt and stepfather; that she must get rid of those poisons before she could be healed of the memory of her parents' murder.

Instead of these cleansings, she threw herself compulsively into trying to help her husband's mentally ill sister. It became almost an obsession that she could heal the sick sister-in-law where doctors had failed.

"I felt I was being sucked down into this abyss, gliding down into this dark world." She thought she, too, was going insane. She couldn't break the identification she had made with the sick woman.

"Finally in desperation I went down on my knees saying 'God help me!' And almost like a billboard— this thing flashed in front of me: 'Leave her alone!' "

It was such a clear command that Sarah followed it. She left the sick sister-in-law alone, stopped having anything to do with her. She even stopped reading the sick woman's wild letters. Her husband and a woman friend tried to help Sarah out of the pit. And she began reading, searching for more about the power that had spoken to her, saying, "Leave her alone!" In a spiritual book which she read one day, she learned that you tie and bind yourself through all Eternity to anyone you hate. As she read this, the thought came sharply:

"I don't want to go through Eternity with my aunt and uncle."

At that second, she forgave them. "I know well it's just the way they were and are. And I refuse to go through Eternity with them. I was freed."

Sarah's release from her years of hatred and wounding came first as a grace, a grace of penitence and forgiveness. Then she put her will to work to continue the forgiveness, the cleansing, every time it came to mind. She then sought help in finding out more about the power so that she could seek its help in other areas of her life.

"My first experience of really feeling that there is a Power that heals, as well as supports you, was in your prayer group," she told me. "Even though I was still shaky from the experiences of years, like a convalescent, I learned in the group that prayer is such a beautiful as well as such a practical, such a real thing. I've never forgotten the talks and sessions we had together. And every day I use prayer—mostly now I thank God. I use prayer for affirming my blessings of which I have so many. And of course my major blessing is the love I have for my family."

What Sarah does not say is how the world sees her, the impression she gave me when we met two or three times a week. She seemed to be one of the best adjusted women in the world. I knew her months before I knew the story of her murdered parents. And not until later did I know of her difficulties with her stepfather, and her failure in trying to help her sister-in-law. I have followed the progress through the years of Sarah and her wonderful husband and her children, who are free of drugs, dropping-out, and other negative syndromes of our time. Sarah, herself, has gone from strength to strength in her mature years. She has united her will with God's grace to cleanse and heal. She has emerged as a light to everyone she meets.

She told me a few years ago:

> Bob is my rock of Gibraltar. He has loved and cherished me for thirty-five years—and no woman ever felt more loved and more secure than I do—and I'm sure that the good Lord certainly gave me enough sense at nineteen to know that this was the right man. As we've both grown and matured, we've grown together—so wonderfully and beautifully, I just feel that I am really probably the most blessed woman in the world.

Sarah's breakthrough from the trauma of her

childhood and the bitterness of her growing years came because she knew the need to forgive, and to cleanse everything that was unlike love, which she later began to call God. When she forgave the people who had hurt her in her childhood, the unclean spirit of bitterness went out of her. The space was filled by the spirit of love which she gives out today not only to her own family but to her fellow workers and her grandchildren. She is walking proof that one can transcend, not just survive, the most extreme tragedy in childhood. This is not a denial of what happened. In fact, even today she says that when watching a western on TV packed with shooting and death, her eyes will suddenly fill with tears. But she brushes them away. She does not dwell on the past.

"Why should I let this thing dominate my life? It's over and done with and I am an extremely fortunate person *now*."

When she said that, she didn't know that another trial lay ahead of her, one that would demand all her faith, one that I'll describe later.

Another friend, Martin, required a more ordinary cleansing than Sarah's drastic one. Hers was almost unique. But Martin's pattern can be found especially in men in every part of our country. Martin had soaked up since childhood the teachings of our society that put power, profits, and property before people. And his *things-before-people* policy succeeded, if you call it success to climb on the backs of others to the top of a power structure. He had almost made it to the top of his company, was vice-president in charge of sales at a Midwest auto plant. For this climb he had sacrificed his family life, especially his fragile, nonexecutive-type wife, Martha. She had to frequent private nursing homes to get over nervous break-downs after years of Martin's alternating neglect and vehement commands that she be a good company hostess. Their two daughters and son grew up really without a father. Martin was always at the plant or off on a business tour abroad. He justified his actions by asserting the all-American goal of wealth and status. After all, he boasted, his children were enroll-ed and registered in the finest schools; his home was huge and in a "good" suburb, decorated as only money can decorate.

He came down to the plant one day, suspecting no change. He learned in the first hour that he was being squeezed out of his job. Not only was the presidency of the plant given to another younger man, but his own job as vice-president was going to go to a man of the new president's choice. He was offered a chance to resign gracefully, but instead chose to stick it out while he found a suitable job elsewhere. With the recession-inflation he couldn't find one. He was too big for a lesser job, his colleagues told him.

On one of his rare talks to himself, he decided that he would chuck the whole thing and do what he had wanted to do as a young man. He would find a job on a college campus teaching. He had a master's degree in history that he had picked up years ago. The only teaching job he could find was in a small junior college in Fort Lauderdale. He put up with the last year of humiliations in order to get every penny due him in salary. But he lost his battle for more stock and a pension.

When Martin and his family came to Florida, he thought he had turned over a new leaf, that he had ditched his power-driven greedy self up north. But during his first two years on campus he not only tried to undercut his academic colleagues, he traded in fast real estate deals on the outside to make extra money to keep his older children in the high-priced colleges they were eager to drop out of. He still never spent any time at home, nor did he pay any more attention to Martha, his wife. His drive was still to put things before people, despite his tiny job as instructor. But he made his wife cut their household expenses to the bone so he could play the market. Martha adjusted well to the new simple life. She didn't have to compete in clothes and hairdos with other executive wives. Nor did she have that old guilt feeling about hating to give company parties. They couldn't afford to entertain even their faculty colleagues. One of the latter invited her to join a prayer group, which is how I met her.

Martha dragged Martin to the group one night. Bristly, bored, and uncomfortable, watching the clock, he almost spoiled the meeting for the rest of us eight men and women. But one man persisted in telling about the cleansing step of breakthrough that we were discussing:

"We tried to cleanse ourselves of our defects through prayer and sharing."

We each told about the old self that we were praying would be killed, to make way for the new life in the spirit. I told of my efforts to combat self-concern and arrogance. Another member told of his attempts to purge himself of temper. Still another, of her attempts to get rid of free-floating anxiety. Martin stopped looking at the clock. In his deep board-meeting voice he spoke up: "I guess even I have a defect—a sort of power drive."

We thanked God that he had this insight. We prayed out loud that God would free Martin of the greed and power drive, and that Martin would cooperate with God in His cleansing work. After that night Martin came regularly to the meetings, and life began to change for him. His marriage seemed to be improving. His campus colleagues liked him better. He even claimed that he was making a real effort to watch and curb the old pattern of "What's in it for me?"

Our prayer group was suspended for the summer since we all went north, east, or west. Martin was left in Florida, where he talked his wife into dipping into her savings account to splurge for a rented house on the beach for the summer. The owner had failed to tell him that on the day they moved in, so would bulldozers, cranes, and cement mixers to build a ten-story condominium next door. The noise blasted Martin's ears from eight o'clock in the morning till four in the afternoon, just when he was trying to write an instant best seller, an account of his life in the auto industry. He fumed each day at the noise. As a result he got little done on the book, and was even too distracted to telephone on his real estate deals. One day he fled the noise to pick up a book at his college library; he bumped into a colleague who happened to be a member of Alcoholics Anonymous. He exploded about his ruined summer to the AA friend who laughed at Martin and said:

"We alcoholics always have to ask ourselves, Is this annoyance worth my taking a drink? Now you're not an alcoholic, but your wife says your blood pressure is way up because of your constant anger. Why not ask yourself if this noise next door is worth a heart attack?"

Martin had to admit that it was not. He found then, as we often do when we probe, that our resentment is usually against ourselves. He had let the old greedy grabber in him cloud his vision in renting what he thought was a summer beach cottage bargain. He had not stopped to examine it. Next he resented the fact that he could not afford just to give up the cottage and lose the rent already paid and move elsewhere. Finally, he was angry at himself for not following his wife's suggestion that they summer cheaply in their own camper, or simply stay at home with occasional weekends away. Though the symptom was resentment, the underlying defect was the same old greed drive.

Once he realized this, he began to admit his powerlessness over the greed and resentment. He even began praying that the Power would cleanse him of it. When the prayer group got going again in the fall, he was actually fitter spiritually than he had ever been in his life. We were then able to help him continue his reconstruction of the new self. Now he had begun to put people, the ones he loved and his colleagues, before things. Responding to the unconditional love we in the prayer group tried to show him, he could begin to see us and then others as "family," not merely as objects to be used or destroyed in a power drive.

Sometimes cleansing or purgation is almost purely passive; that is, it is forced on you by circumstances over which you have little control. Your part in it is to try to find meaning in the suffering and to use it to be transformed by God.

This was the case of my mother. Through no fault of her own, no defect on her part, she had a long, hard battle with genteel poverty while trying to raise the children according to her own high standards. The Depression merely made things worse. I contributed to her anguish by my life as a wild young alcoholic, and later by my cold rejection of her. Mother survived all these hardships into her mid-fifties, for she was both courageous and resilient. Then a particularly painful type of arthritis began to cripple her from the hips down. She tried everything medicine offered to alleviate the pain. But it increased as the arthritis spread.

Then she began to learn that whenever she gave in-to rebellion against the pain, or succumbed to fear of the future, frustration at the present, or resentment of the past, her pain became far worse. She began taking an active role in cleansing; she began praying to the Lord to remove the negatives, the thoughts that crowded unwanted into her solitary hotel room. She began turning outward, out of herself up to God, and then out to others.

Though tied to her chair or her walker, she spent hours each day in prayer for others, and in so doing forgot her own pain. She was even able to banish the memories of those exhausting earlier years. In her eighties she attained a "widespreading love to all in common." Her love embraced in active concern young drug addicts, the poor with whom she could identify easily, and any other sufferers. She turned from her own prison of pain to the pain of the planet and the suffering of her fellow sojourners on the spaceship earth.

Gifted with a young mind, she helped me enormously in my writing, not only by inspiration and suggestions, but by her total recall of facts from my childhood that I needed. Despite her pain, her old age became illumined by love in action and prayer for others. Her cleansing was almost complete. She had moved on in her maturity to the stage of illumination, a life of prayer and works. She had found a Model to follow, the living Lord in whom she had come to believe.

Each of us is given light on what we are meant to be, or what God wants us to be, if we have followed through on our own cleansing. These glimpses or images generally come to us during the struggle to clean up the old self. The vision of the new self, and its seeming realization in our lives, called the illuminative stage, is a very happy one. But we need models, or I would say a Model, that will help us become the best that we are.

Tools for Cleansing

1. Make a breakthrough from what you are to what God wants you to be.
2. If you don't take the initiative in cleansing, it will take you.
3. Don't try to go it alone. Share in a fellowship with others who are consciously moving from the kinship of suffering, through survival to transcendence.
4. Each one reach one.
5. You are helped where you hurt.
6. Choose the major defect that is hampering you and let it go one day at a time, practicing custody of the heart.
7. Kick the pattern of problem addiction.
8. Try to cleanse yourself of your defects through prayer and sharing.

The Seven Stages of Breakthrough—
From Survival to Transcendence

1. ADMISSION AND AWAKENING
We admitted we were powerless over our suffering and/or our particular defect that is keeping us from making a breakthrough from what we are to what God wants us to be, and that only God can help us to survive.

2. PRAYER
We sought through prayer, meditation, and contemplation to improve our spontaneous communication with God. We carried on a dialogue with God, replacing the old "monologue with me."

3. CLEANSING
We tried to cleanse ourselves of our defects through prayer and sharing.

4. ILLUMINATION
We obtained a glimpse of the best that we are, the image of what God intends us to be.

5. THE DARK NIGHT OF THE SOUL
We reached a turning point in which the old divided self battled with the emerging new self. Resistance to breakthrough is stubborn.

6. SURRENDER
We surrendered ourselves to God, moment by moment, seeking the state of abandonment to God as a way of life.

7. THE UNITIVE STATE
While making our own breakthrough, we carried the message, person to person and to the wider community, practicing these principles in all our affairs, one day at a time.

Chapter 4

Be the Best That You Are

Out on the reef my glass mask has for years enabled me to see not only the barracuda, but also to view the beauties of the underwater world. And on shore, as far back as the 1950s, while my defects began to be purged, I was also receiving tools to cleanse the doors of my perception. These tools I called "survival sentences." They began floating to mind a few months after my husband, Jack Lewis, and I moved to Jamaica in the West Indies. The sentences were simultaneous with the cleansing process. They were like the beautiful parrot fish or gleaming silvery tarpon of the underwater world, so entrancing that they kept me from forsaking that world because of its dangers. On land they kept me from regressing to a state of complacency with surface, secular experiences only, experiences in which my perception could have been once more blinded to the beauty I had glimpsed.

The survival sentences were more than that. They were actually tools for transcending suffering. They helped me rise above and beyond problems, even if only for months. In this they were like the golden shafts of sunlight spotlighting the ocean bottom. They were a foretaste of what is called the illuminative state, the state in which you pause on a plateau of joy, of quiet exaltation, on the spiraling journey of the spirit. These sentences even began to form a composite image of a model, a model who was the exemplar of what I would try to become.

The first survival sentence came to help me in 1954, a month after Jack and I had begun our new life on our beat-up, newly bought plantation, Rose Hill, Runaway Bay in Jamaica. One hot August day in the chaos of crop time, I stood on the verandah wishing for wings so that I could fly the two miles from our hilltop home to the sea beneath us. I had no wings so I tried instead to glance at a book, *Men Who Have Walked with God*, by Sheldon Cheney (Knopf, 1948). It told of Brother Lawrence and St. Francis and others who sought and found the presence of God within them.

My eyes turned from the book to look again at the turquoise Caribbean, stretched beneath me in smiling repose, out through the serene green and gold cane fields in the blazing sun. Closer were the mauve-trunked coconut trees, and next to the house the geometric shapes of the shiny waxen green leaves of breadfruit trees. I became quiet amidst the hammering of carpenters on the shingled roof and the slapping of masons' trowels on the bathroom floor and concrete drying barbecues. I became quiet for the first time since our Jamaica journey had begun two months earlier. And out of that quiet came the question:

"What would I like more than anything else in the world if I could have my heart's desire?"

The answers tattooed back: an iced coffee, a hot shower, electric lights, a road to the sea, so I could swim, and to the north coast resorts where there would be people to talk to and not just black cattle.

I stopped my demands because another desire, totally unheralded, floated to consciousness:

"What I really want is not just these things. What I

really want is to *be a saint with a sense of humor.*"

I said it out loud. I spoke it out on the verandah, high over the Caribbean, to the sun, to the sea, to the green, green trees. "I want to be a saint with a sense of humor."

I didn't know what a saint was. I guessed that a saint wouldn't be fretting about discomforts of an old farm such as rats, bats, mosquitoes, sand flies, and lack of ice, lights, or hot water. A saint was, perhaps, a person who was good, a saint was one who was loving. And a sense of humor, that I knew—a sense of humor gives perspective on the present. A saint with a sense of humor. I liked the sound of it, and what's more I seemed to like the goal of it. For if I were a saint I would be a good and loving woman who could laugh not only at my foibles of ten years ago, but at myself today, right here and now as I stood in the unaccustomed role of "missus" of a Jamaica plantation.

And then I did laugh. I laughed at the sheer presumption of the goal to be a saint with a sense of humor, as I remembered the broad road I had traveled from Greenwich Village drinking days to this plantation in the West Indies in 1954. How wild can you be, I asked myself, to consider such a goal? Ask my psychoanalyst who knew all my secrets laid bare on his couch. Ask those I had hurt while drinking and even those I had hurt since I stopped drinking. Ask that handful who knew of the deed I had performed— a deed I will shortly describe—a deed some considered patriotic, but one that my conscience knew was the greatest sin I had ever committed. I could hear the scornful laughter of psychoanalysts, bartenders, lovers, relatives, and one-time friends.

Survival Kit

I buried the survival sentence "to be a saint with a sense of humor" under the frenzied rush of crop time, the threats of Hurricane Hazel at which we ran to board up and batten down, the predawn journeys by Land Rover to fetch our allspice pickers.

The goal was buried under the nightmare that began when my sin of the previous year suddenly boomeranged onto the verandah of Rose Hill threatening to rip me away from my new husband, my new life, my new home. My sin had been to go to the FBI. I did it when my then fiancé, a naval officer, insisted that I make this last ditch attempt to get "cleared" so that the Navy would let him marry me, would lift the ban that they had ordered on the eve of our wedding. The Navy had alleged that my leftwing past made me "dangerous," that I therefore could not marry a naval officer. My fiancé after trying to get the ban lifted at the highest Washington levels, said that our only chance was for me to go to the FBI and "make a clean breast" of my youthful activism in the left.

In a state of mental and physical collapse I did what he asked. The awful act did not, of course, have the slightest effect on our situation. He was instead speedily posted to a no-woman base thousands of miles away and soon he had forgotten me and our hopeless future and married another.

Then, in 1954, a representative of the American Department of Justice arrived unannounced on our verandah, first asked me, and then threatened to subpoena me, to come back and testify (during the McCarthy madness of those days) not about myself, but about other people I might have known ten or fourteen years earlier. Next they threatened to insist that Jamaica deport me permanently if I would not comply with their demand. After that, they threatened to bar my British husband from ever returning to America, so that we would never see each other again.

The terror by night and by noonday led me to take an oath to the queen to prevent my deportation by Jamaica from the island and my husband. Now I fought only for survival and sanity. Now I was a virtual exile from my native America, since I was told that I would be subpoenaed again should I put foot in America. Once subpoenaed, I would share the fate of others who could not testify about their acquaintances or friends. I would be sent to jail for contempt.

Exiled on my island paradise with the haunting knowledge that I could not go home again, I survived by throwing myself into the motor-minded work I knew best, reporting. I forgot all about that goal of becoming a saint with a sense of humor. I never even looked up what the definition of a saint might be. I had in fact to climb Jamaica's highest peak, Blue Mountain, at midnight, through rain and mud and cold, and to hear the piercing primeval song of the solitaire bird, before I even remembered that, two years earlier, I had briefly glimpsed a goal, to be a saint with a sense of humor.

The thick mist of clouds prevented our seeing the sunrise from the peak. We settled halfway down the mountain in a hostel. There I did find a sunrise, one that would illumine my entire life. For in that remote hostel was a book, begrimed by the sticky fingers of hikers, riddled with inch-deep holes eaten by bookworms, and mildewed by years of mountain mist. Its words stood out in gold. This book was William James' masterpiece, *The Varieties of*

Religious Experience (Modern Library, n.d.).

And in this book by America's pioneer psychologist-philosopher was the word, not once, but many times, "saint." He defined a saint as ". . .the character for which spiritual emotions are the habitual centre of the personal energy. . ."

Excitedly I read on that night by kerosene lamp. Did he tell how to become a saint? Did he tell how to learn to dwell on the inner spiritual life and not solely on the outer life of exile, the externals of the latest news story, of crop failures, frustrations at not having a baby, fear of the overdraft at the bank? Here perhaps in this old, wormeaten book was an answer. There wasn't time to read the five hundred pages that night. I had to wait until my own copy arrived from America. Then I sat down with pen in hand and devoured it as I read it for the first of many times. For in it lay the perfectly documented, beautifully written experiences of those souls who, since the beginning of recorded history, had embarked on the journey of the spirit, under an Indian bo tree, in an ancient Chinese garden, in medieval Cologne, France, England, Italy, and Spain.

Their walk with God began not only in monasteries, convents, or churches, but also in poverty-stricken artists' studios, on poets' writing tables, in scholars' libraries, at cobblers' benches, and, yes, in housewives' kitchens. Presented for me to ponder were St. Paul, St. Francis, George Fox, William Blake, Meister Eckhart, St. Teresa of Avila, Walt Whitman, Blaise Pascal, Jacob Boehme, Mme. Guyon, and many others of Eastern as well as Western religions.

Most of the great ones described by James were at

first divided souls, rent with inner conflicts, seeking survival itself. Then, while strolling in an English lane, or in the midst of fitful sleep, or standing in the village square, the gray caul of suffering was lifted long enough to cleanse their vision, to let the light shine around about them, illuminating their world and showing them not only what the world should be, but showing them what they should be, a glimpse of God, the best that they were, the image of a new self that transcended the old divided self. But who was the model for that new self that I was looking for? That I didn't know and couldn't seem to find in James' book.

Was it someone like the stranger who had seemed to appear one early morning as I stood again on Rose Hill verandah? Then I had seemed to see a figure walking lightly and swiftly not on but above the steep driveway of the front common. As he came nearer, I could see his face, I thought, loving, luminous, tender. He seemed to walk right up to the verandah, to stand beside me, point out the vast expanse of sea to the north, to the east, and to the west of us, saying:

All good comes your way on the Island of To-day.
Nothing can board your Island, save you give it entry at the port of your heart.
You can bar or deport all those enemies—of your own household—
Just as you can bar hostile ships or planes.
Take therefore no thought for the morrow; for the morrow shall take thought for the things of itself.
Sufficient for you it is to live on the Island of To-day.

And then he vanished, leaving an afterglow that led me swiftly to write down those words: *"Live on the Island of Today."* Banish the fears of reprisal, fears of the future; bar the past and live just for this day. I meditated on this survival sentence before my day's work covering celebrities, tourists, and natives on the Gold Coast. I savored each word that had been given to me, mulling them over, feasting on the words, pondering their meaning for me.

I had quite simply been lifted by that vision, from the prayer of petition only, to the stage beyond petition, meditation. *Now I practiced giving my time, skill, energy, and attention to words and sentences as they came, till they revealed their meaning to me.* My previous prayers of petition had been mostly me, with very little God in them. Meditation was less of me, and more of God. And the more time I gave to meditation, the more often the survival sentences came. They happened when I walked on Rose Hill's highest slope, or lazed suspended under water snorkeling, or simply driving on my beat along the North Coast cane fields, towns, and harbors.

One day at the season's peak in Jamaica, I slowed my reporter's pace to spend ten minutes watching a very tall man whose name I never learned but who impressed me more than almost all the celebrities I covered for the Associated Press and the Jamaica *Daily Gleaner* in my six years on the island.

I immediately called him "The Man on the White River Bridge." I first spotted him as I slowed down to make it over the one-lane, wooden bridge that then spanned the river. Fascinated, I drove over to the far side of the river where I could continue to watch him unobserved.

It certainly was not his clothes or even his great height that stopped me. His sunburned pink, bald head, his knee-length shorts taut over his slight pot belly, his multi-colored madras shirt, and the camera over his shoulder marked him as just one of thousands of ordinary American tourists.

What stopped me was the extraordinary expression on his rather ordinary face. He was gazing with the eyes of ardent love up the banana-banked, white sand-bottomed river that flowed out to the sea. His face was lighted by that rare quality in today's world, the quality of pure joy, as he looked at the cottontree dugout canoes with their black-skinned owners gleaming in the sunlight. He seemed transfixed and transfigured in a sort of selfless childlike delight. He was, in fact, the moment I glimpsed him, *having a love affair with life.*

I wanted to leap out of the car and tell him that he could, if he chose, *make every day a holiday*, even back at the office Monday. He could do this; he had proven right on the bridge that he already had one tool to use, the tool of meditation that I had just started practicing in the forest, underwater, and in my car. But I didn't tell him this. I realized as I drove away that "The Man on the White River Bridge" would probably act like the scores of other tourists whose flights from the island I had reported. He would check that tool for transcending, that tool of meditation, at the baggage counter of the airport. He would in fact leave behind any and all tools for transcending difficulties of suffering. We seem to pick them up and use them only once a year, on our vacations. He would, like most of us, relegate the meditative joy on the bridge to the realm of pure chance.

Yet the very fact that he and you and I have been able to *free ourselves of the finite and immerse ourselves in the infinite* for even seconds on holidays indicates, does it not, that we could, if wc tried make at least some part of each day a holiday, set aside an oasis in each day for pure childlike joy and meditation?

You have glimpsed this joy on your own holiday when you raised your eyes to praise the grace of gannets plummeting and soaring over the cliffs of the Gaspé Peninsula.

You have glimpsed it when you looked against the sun at the sky matching the sea over the white sail of your boat at the Cape.

You have glimpsed it as you rode horseback or walked in the dappled sunlight filtering through the tall pines of the green-gauzed forest on Mackinac Island.

You have glimpsed it when you strolled in quiet exaltation under moss-draped live oak trees in an ancient church yard at Sea Island, Georgia.

"The Man on the White River Bridge" prodded me to search for others who used tools that could make every day a holiday. I started my quest among the American tourists I interviewed for my reporter's beat. On their brief holidays they were using several tools. Then I turned to study the people not on holiday, the working people, and especially those who worked for us on our ancient farm.

I found a man and a woman who, though poles apart in their stations in life, both used tools that did indeed make every day a holiday. I didn't have to look far for the woman. She lived and worked right on our farm. Tiny, black, plump, and middle-aged, she was my cook, Lillian Buckle. Plagued with backache, earning only a few pounds sterling each week, deserted by her man, worried about her grandchildren, Lillian was the living example of a saint with a sense of humor. She became my guide in my quest, for she had arrived at the illuminative stage of spiritual life, practicing both prayer and love-in-action.

Cooking on a stove too high for her tiny stature, standing at a sink too tall for her, she also slept in crowded staff quarters with noisy cattlemen and the allspice pickers. Yet Lillian showed me by her attitude and actions how to *make every day a holiday*, despite the turmoil of the life of her "Missus," me, the over-aged American bride, and the turbulent atmosphere generated by Jack.

My other guide stood at the opposite end of the spectrum. He was an internationally renowned lawyer, a scholar, and a noted speaker. I first met Louis Nizer when I interviewed him on holiday at Jamaica Inn, Ocho Rios. I was much impressed by his ability to abandon himself to childlike joy in drawing caricatures, writing children's songs, golfing, and giving his time to others. I wired in a full column about him for my paper. I did not include in the story, however, my secret reservations about him, namely that it is all good and well to be so full of joy on holiday, but what is he like back at the office Monday? Will he stand that test? How will he act under pressure? Nor did I realize that I would find out in a situation that would originate with my own legal problem carried to his New York office.

But back in Jamaica, Louis Nizer gave me another

tool for my kit. I called it: *be the best that you are*. He was always large-hearted, large-spirited, generous in pouring himself out for others. He was in fact the person you become when you board the plane, car, or bus for your own holiday. You peel off the casement of your office skin, revealing the outgoing childlike spirit underneath. You *become the best that you are*—magnanimous, lofty in spirit. Out of your own freedom and joy you practice *each one reach one*, in helping a fellow traveler with a flat tire, or a mother who needs to warm a bottle for her baby. Everything in you is up and out, turned outward toward other people, not down, not turned inward on yourself.

Being the best that you are is not limited to holidayers, Lillian proved to me at Rose Hill. She showed this same expansiveness of spirit, cooking over the too-high stove, washing dishes at the too-tall sink, every working day of the year. She was the best that she could be in her humble job. She enjoyed the appreciation of our guests who asked for seconds of her tasty shrimp soup (it had twenty two ingredients!) and her limeade blended from our limes, fresh ginger, and rich black head sugar. It quenched more than our physical thirst. And each Thursday, the day before market day, Lillian came to tell me the cupboard was bare. There was, she said, not a thing to make for dinner.

I said, "Do the best you can," smiling as I turned back to the typewriter. For I knew that Thursday night would be a special feast. Her "make-do" dinner consisted of salt fish and ackee—salt fish from her own supplies stored in her room, ackee from our trees—with homegrown avocadoes and her special herb, oil, and vinegar dressing. Dessert was sometimes mangoes with her special hard sauce made of coconuts fresh from the trees.

I missed Lillian when my husband and I flew overseas for a long trip. But we went with her prayers for the baby we hoped to adopt and bring back to the farm. Months later when we came home and drove up the steep and winding white marl lane, Lillian was waiting for us, standing in front of the kitchen, her black face smiling, her brown eyes dancing, her arms out ready to receive the young and growing life that she wanted as much as I did. She ran forward as I got out of the car. Then she stopped, frowned, raised her eyebrows. She saw that my arms were empty. She ran forward again now to hug me as though to fill the emptiness. Then she led me up the stone steps onto the verandah. She poured out a glass of her limeade. She stood by me while I drank it, patting my shoulder, saying:

"Miss Sue, perhaps God means you to keep on helping them grown-ups that you try to help. Maybe they have to be your children—not a baby. Just trust Him and thank Him anyways."

I couldn't thank Him that day or the next. But Lillian thanked Him for me, showing me how to *make gratitude your attitude*. She acted and spoke as if *everything is gravy*. Each day she knocked on my door with my early morning coffee tray, flung the door open revealing the splendor of the hedge of red and yellow hibiscus lightly veiling the sea beneath and beyond, the green angular-shaped leaves of the breadfruit trees, and the white swirled trunks of the allspice trees topped with their jade foliage.

"Praise the Lord for this beautiful day, for this is the day the Lord has made!" Then, smiling slyly, she added, "Just be glad you're not one of them rich folks up North working to make money in all that cold and snow so they can come down here for just a week. Be glad you live here."

The night the fire broke out at Rose Hill, leaping from our neighbor's sugar cane fields, it was Lillian who rode with me while I raced the Land Rover five miles down the hill to round up villagers to man a bucket brigade. Jack was away. It was Lillian who kept the coffeepot going, the limeade laced with a tot of rum. She carried endless trays out to the men and women who formed a chain to fight the fire crackling and burning to the ground the dry trees and fence-posts. Lillian led us in singing the old Jamaican work chants and some hymns as we loped back and forth scores of times from the fast diminishing rainwater tank. Her spirit lifted ours so that we could make a game of the deadly sport of fire fighting. And at dawn when we had finally quenched the fire only a few feet from the house, Lillian smiled as we rocked, and said, "We won, Miss Sue, God and we won. We can do all things through Christ who strengthens us."

If we could make a game of the terror of that night, we could *make a game of almost anything*, I realized as I pondered this new tool Lillian had added to the survival kit. Sportsmanship need not be relegated to holiday scuba diving expeditions down among the sharks, barracuda, and moray eels; or trying a fence too high for you on a hard-to-handle horse. We are such good sports on holiday, and we do *make a game of everything*, late planes, bad weather, even injuries gotten on tennis courts, swimming, riding, or walking. We transcend anything that happens, viewing our vicissitudes as a challenge, as an adventure.

Is good sportsmanship a tool we can really carry back to the office Monday? I wondered later as I waited to see Louis Nizer in his big law suite on Broadway. Could even Lou help me make a game of the ugly piece of paper—a new subpoena—stemming from my old activist days? Or would Lou in his native habitat be another person, too preoccupied, too hard-pressed to show the contagious high spirits of his Jamaican holiday self? I had been advised that now I *could* come home again, that McCarthyism was dead and I had nothing to fear at the hands of committees. But the subpoena had been served on me the night before, just days after my arrival in the United States for a reunion with my family.

My heart sank as I entered his private office. The distance from the door seemed to stretch miles across a thick blue carpet to his massive desk. Behind it sat Louis Nizer, his beautiful head bent over some papers. I almost turned and ran.

But then Lou looked up, and there spread over his face the familiar near-beatific smile. He stood and hugged me. Then he showed me the paper he had been so intent upon. It was a caricature he had sketched as I approached him. It was such a funny take-off on the worry and down lines of my face that I laughed at it and, more important, I laughed at me. After he seated me, he asked me in his soft voice about our good friends in Jamaica. But when he got to the details of the new subpoena I began to machine gun my recitation of the facts. He, in turn, became slower and slower in the enunciation of his questions. I laughed again, remembering our very first interview back in Jamaica. He had said then:

"When the pressure is greatest—that's when I go into slow motion, in talking, in writing, even in picking up the phone."

By the time he had finished eliciting the facts, his relaxed manner had me almost lolling in the soft deep chair. He rang for an assistant, spoke a few quiet words to him. He then took me strolling past his collection of paintings and books, smiling in his happy fashion. His wife Mildred had once told me, "To Lou every day is his birthday."

When Lou outlined what he had already set in motion to help me, I knew that he had begun a love affair with my case with his whole heart. And with his whole mind he had penetrated the legal intricacies, because he is always the best that he is. Besides he loves his work. He had told me once:

"Nothing is work unless you'd rather be doing something else."

As he showed me out of his office, he said, "Sue, you have handed your problem over to me. It is my job from now on. But you also have a job to do while you wait for my call tonight or tomorrow morning."

I expected him to tell me to go back to the apartment and write down long pages of facts on my case, rehearsing the poison and the pain of it. Instead he said:

"Go on out to an art gallery—or a movie—forget the case. After all, this day is still part of your vacation. Make it a holiday. Do something that gives you some joy. And then do something that gives joy to someone else."

I walked out onto Broadway realizing that while Louis Nizer had been helping me survive this anxious day and night, he had also proved that he was the same man back at the office Monday as he was on

holiday. He had *made a game of everything*. He had
certainly practiced *each one reach one* by giving his
whole time to me. And he had started his love affair
with my case even before I left the office. I felt I owed
him at least the response of doing what he suggested,
to try to make this day a holiday. And since nothing
makes me feel freer than taking an afternoon off for a
movie, I did just that. I threw myself into a plush seat
of an upper east side movie house. I feasted on the
paintings of Vincent Van Gogh in the old film *Lust for
Life*. I freed myself from the finite worries of my case
by immersing myself in the infinite, the masterpieces,
and the story of a great artist.

But as I left the theater in the late afternoon rush, I
felt a distinct dip in spirit. It hit me even as did the
cold air, and the fact of the long night's waiting for
Lou's word on my fate. Fear flooded back and with it
envy of the hurrying homebound crowds. They had
homes. They knew where they'd be tomorrow, and a
year from now. I was in legal limbo between my
beloved Jamaica two thousand miles to the south, and
this northern island of Manhattan. The government
said I had lost my right to be one of the hurrying,
homebound American citizens. And I silently screamed the word "alien," trapped as I felt in the prison of
legal reprisals, and the equally confining prison of my
fear.

How would I get through the rest of the night
alone? Yet I needed to be alone for Lou's call, for
answering any questions, and for thinking. Tendrils
of anxiety sprouted out in my mind as I completely
forgot the tools of the survival kit. Descending into
the inferno of the roaring subway I couldn't transcend
my problem. Even survival seemed difficult as the

crowd pushed me out at my stop and buffeted me toward the steep stairs to the street. My tropics-acclimated body shivered at Manhattan's cold wind cutting me as I walked toward the apartment.

So concerned with me was I that I bumped into a very tall, bald man who was standing still on the curb, even though the light was with us. I had already started to rush past him when he said apologetically:

"I wonder if you would be so kind as to help me across? I am a little confused. I just got my new glasses—wearing them the first time since my cataract surgery."

While I was holding the elbow of the big but helpless man, guiding him across the busy avenue, the night seemed less cold. It felt, in fact, crisp and bracing. He thanked me profusely as I took him to his nearby apartment entrance. And as I said good-bye, I remembered that other tall and bald-headed man, the one who had stood transfixed with the vision of beauty before him, "The Man on the White River Bridge," on that distant afternoon. How lucky he was, in fact, how lucky I was, that we could see so clearly the colors, the beauty, and the light of the world. I looked up at the dark towering masses of stone hiding the sky. But even as I looked, the lights twinkled on in the windows like the stars turning on in the black night over Rose Hill. I muttered a thank-you that I could see both twinkling lights and stars, and that I could walk free without tripping. My steps lightened as I neared the apartment, for I realized that in spite of my self-concern, the tall, bald man on this northern island had helped me recover the tools for transcending, by letting me help him. And he had helped me recover the tool I had mislaid altogether, the practice of gratitude—that my dear Lillian had taught me during those early mornings in Jamaica. But she had really given me far more than tools to make every day a holiday. She had given me tools to make every day a *holy day*—the original meaning of the word holiday.

Now I no longer dreaded the long night's wait. The hours fell into a sequence of love-in-action and prayer, beginning with that delayed letter I would write to Lillian. I had a lot of thanksgiving to do, thanking people as well as thanking God. I took out my key and opened the door. Then I sat down at my typewriter and began my letter to Lillian. And as I did so, I started in a very small way to *make this day a holy day.*

I kept the goal before me during the endless days, then weeks of waiting to be released from the subpoena. Finally I was set free to go back to the farm in Jamaica. Surrounded by Lillian and friends, I was happy to resume my married life and my reporting. But the hot center of my attention focused on finding tools to become the best that I could be, that is, to make every day a holy day. I sensed that my Jamaica journey was reaching some kind of climax. Two years later it did. It came to a screeching halt.

My ailing marriage, already weakened by the strains of subpoenas, exile, and interrogations, finally sickened and died. My husband had taken as much as he could with me. He found someone else with a less turbulent life. Now I was forced to leave the bright and shining island for sheer escape from his threats. And I came home again, but now as an alien in my own land, with a three-month visitors' visa stamped in the dark blue British passport.

I did not feel alone even though I was a solitary sojourner to the States. I seemed to be following an invisible leader who would show me more than the fleeting glimpses of God I had received during the six-year Jamaica journey. Obediently I followed the leader until at summer's end I found myself in the only room I could afford, a room at the San Diego YWCA. Now I was stripped of marriage and citizenship in my country, and stripped of the right to work by immigration authorities.

In that little upper room of the YWCA I met the invisible leader face to face in a split and blinding second. He came before me saying:

"I am God. Before Abraham was, I am."

He said, "Come unto me . . . and I will give you rest."

I answered, "Yes, Lord, yes." For I knew in that instant that Jesus was God, not merely man, and that He was my Savior. Though totally insecure in my material life, I became blissfully secure in my interior self. In having Jesus Christ as Lord, I knew I had everything. My love affair with the Lord began at that moment. I devoured His word in the gospels, especially his command:

Seek ye first the Kingdom of God, and his righteousness; and all these things shall be added unto you. (Matthew 6:33)

This meant to me first that I must become part of His spiritual kingdom, that I must stabilize my relationship with Jesus. I joined His body in the Catholic church. It was a church my human mind would not have chosen. My centuries-old Protestant, Quaker family—those centuries of liberal crusaders—were contrary to the then Roman Catholic church. But I followed Christ's lead to Rome since I had told Him I wanted to go all the way.

The kingdom of God also meant to me my earthly kingdom, the United States. I prayed constantly for repatriation in my own land. I was in limbo, rejected by my country, yet fearing to go back to Jamaica and the frightening atmosphere generated by Jack.

I received an answer to my prayer, given by a tiny, black-eyed South Korean lady, Mme. Induk Pahk. I listened to her as she spoke at the hotel in Arizona where I was then being housed by friends while waiting for action on my citizenship. In the first minutes of her talk, I realized that she was a woman of prayer. Her whole life work had been built on prayer, raising funds to build a school for educating young South Koreans. After her talk I went to her cottage at the hotel. Soon I was pouring out my fears of deportation when my final extension of my visa expired.

By one of those "coincidences" in the life of the spirit, she told me of her own struggle to stay in America, where she felt she could do most to raise funds for her dreamed-of school. She had prayed not to be deported, but to win residence here. The answer to her prayer was a congressman who introduced a private bill that would grant her status as a permanent resident, free to stay as long as she wished. She mobilized all her prayer partners to win the bill's passage. On the very day that she would have been deported, their prayers were answered. She won her permanent residence.

She wouldn't listen to my objections that I had no friend at court to help me. Instead she made me pray with her that God would help me as He had helped

83

her. She also told me of her amazing experience in learning to surrender—an experience I was not ready to absorb at that time.

But I was ready to be helped on my citizenship. The next morning, instead of talking or writing to God as I usually did, I listened. His answer might have seemed foolish to the world. But I was compelled to act as He asked. I wrote my hometown congressman, Francis E. Walter, asking for his help. He seemed the least likely person in the country to sponsor me, for he was chairman of the notorious House Un-American Activities Committee that had begun making my life miserable as far back as 1941. He was, however, also chairman of the House subcommittee on immigration. By one of those "miracles," instead of turning me down, for I had been in my youth one of the group he hated most (liberal, activist, progressive), he actually introduced a private bill that would restore my citizenship rights exactly as they had been before my oath to the queen. As long as the bill was not voted down, I could stay; I could even work, immigration officials told me.

Now I could do the only thing that I wanted to do. I could support myself while studying what Jesus had said about the kingdom of God, His word, and His work. I prayed that He would send me south where I could study theology. He took me literally and sent me to *South* Bend, one of the centers of the snow belt in Indiana. I began four years of work and study at the age of forty-five, the most arduous I had ever known. But when you are in love you do not get tired. Your love gives you unlimited energy. And then He gave me a further gift.

One early morning in October, 1961, shortly after I

had arrived at South Bend, I knelt at the communion rail in urgent prayer, the last of many prayers for courage to undergo upcoming surgery. I admitted the failure of my own prayers. I simply gave up. Then it was that the Holy Spirit prayed in me. He prayed in a way least expected, giving me a completely formed poem, a rhyming prayer that I had nothing to do with. I had never even tried to write a poem. Now I was serving as amanuensis for the Spirit as the words became lines and the lines formed a verse. All I did was type it out when I returned to my room.

The prayer-poem marked my infilling by the Holy Spirit, an active sense of His presence, two months after my confirmation. His greatest gift that morning was the onset of contemplative prayer, "the tasting knowledge of God." In addition, though I wouldn't know this until six years later, He had given me a charismatic way of praying in the Holy Spirit.

This first prayer poem has since been printed in anthologies, newspapers, on cards and in newsletters. It is carried in wallets and purses by many survivors and transcenders. Of myself, I could not have written it, nor could I attain the high goal it sets.

> Lord, empty me of me,
> That I may fill up with Thee.
>
> Every minute I've spent on me,
> Lord, I now dedicate to Thee.
>
> The more the world takes from me,
> The more will I produce for Thee.
>
> The more perfect my confidence in Thee,
> The more special Thy Providence to me.

> And whatever may happen to me,
> I say, Blessed be the Name of Thee.

I was, with this prayer, being offered the gift of surrender, the greatest gift in the life of prayer. I accepted it gratefully, and temporarily. As if in response, I was showered with prayer-poems. They were all entirely involuntary. They floated into form when I stood on a cold South Bend street corner waiting for the bus, or rode the bus out to Saint Mary's. They came in the classroom where I sat with thirty classmates, nuns studying theology and scripture. They came to me in my bare rather gloomy office where I earned my salary as dean of students at the Holy Cross Nursing School. Or they came in my dormitory room, despite the noise of two hundred teen-age nursing students.

Each prayer-poem came when I *needed* it, not when I wanted it. I could never force or induce a verse. All I did was receive it with the pen of a rapid writer and a notebook. Some actually brought light on the fruits of the Holy Spirit. And one showed me a tool that had lain rusting in my survival kit, and now came to help me.

Despite the progress I made in Mismated Anonymous at conquering my pattern of addiction to men, the old temptation showed up soon after I came to South Bend. He was a very handsome and a very good man. But he was a married man with children. I spent eighteen months trying to resist him and to root out my unfulfilled passion. I spent hours in prayer trying to combat him, but just as many hours daydreaming about him. Finally I flew to a distant city and made a five-day retreat to get away from all sight or thought of him. In the confessional I confided to an old English Benedictine priest. He listened in the hot little box, then said with a smile in his voice:

"My dear, you'll have these temptations until they carry you out feet first. Do not feel guilty about them. Just don't give in to them. Hand them over to the Lord."

I did hand my passion over to the Lord. And this time He did free me, in a totally unexpected way. He gave me a sense of humor about it, through a poem He called, "Lines to My Lord from a Three-Time Loser"—a verse that poked fun at the whole ridiculous situation of Susan the middle-aged convert-divorcée panting like a school girl after a middle-aged married man. As the verse rolled out, it lifted the pressure of my unfulfilled sex drive and later transformed the relationship to a good, solid friendship. I could at last laugh at myself, a very good protection against temptation.

Four years of joyous illumination followed my encounter with the Holy Spirit. They were years filled with praising the Lord, plus study, praising the Lord, plus work, praising the Lord, plus the apostolate. The Holy Spirit seemed to activate and increase my person-to-person rescue work, not only with alcoholics, but with all kinds of people in trouble. I responded, grateful that I could try to give back what had so graciously been given me. And I was even blessed with the holy guidance of my spiritual director, Father Putz, who had made it possible for me to come to South Bend and work and study, by finding me a job and opening the academic doors for me.

So spirit-filled was I in those years at Saint Mary's that I was only bothered by the continuing rejection of my country, when an event requiring action took place. I could almost forget that I was living on borrowed time in America, that tomorrow I might be sent into permanent exile. One of my prayer partners, with whom I shared my thoughts, especially when I had to be fingerprinted every two years, was an English-born nurse, Anne. She was more than a friend; she was, like Lillian, an example of the illuminative stage of the journey. She combined the life of prayer with the life of love-in-action, pouring herself out in hard physical work to all who asked. Even after long days of nursing on the wards, she gave her free time to babysitting, cleaning house, and helping in moving for her friends. Her attitude was gratitude, and gratitude is the beginning of humility, and humility of course is the highway to holiness, to making every day a holy day. She seemed grateful for the gift of life itself. Her sense of humor lighted up the dormitory, the wards, or a party.

She was, however, far too wise in the way of the spirit to mistake her illuminated state for the final goal of the journey. She feasted while she could, knowing that famine might well lie ahead, as it does for all who want to go all the way. I was not so wise. I mistook this marvelous love affair with the Lord, the illuminative stage, for the highest peak of the mountain. I thought I had arrived at the unitive state, that I needed no further tools in the survival kit. I was encouraged in this illusion by the rewards of those four years of hard work.

On a day in August, 1965, I walked to the stage of Saint Mary's O'Laughlin Auditorium and in glory received my doctorate in theology. I was publicized and praised not only for teaching the first spontaneous prayer course given in a college that summer to priests, nuns, and laymen, but hailed for launching the first spontaneous prayer conference in the Catholic church. As I traveled away from South Bend, I wrote a prayer-poem at the Holy Spirit's dictation, dedicating myself anew to Him, "The Time That Is Left Belongs Solely to You." Then I journeyed south in hope and joy for my first full-time teaching job at Marymount College, Boca Raton, Florida. At last I was back by my beloved southern sea. In fact, I was lucky enough to rent a cottage just two blocks from the ocean. I christened it and had it blessed as "Case de la Paloma," House of the Dove, in honor of the Holy Spirit.

I had failed to heed the warnings of my dead and living companions of the spirit. I thought the sun-filled meadow of illumination was the sign of my spirtual marriage to Jesus, the seal of my permanent union with Him. Not only had I survived the sufferings of the past, I was transcending my trouble of the present, the deportation threat, should the bill be killed in Congress. Now I could bask in the presence of God in well-earned stable surcease from the devils of dubious excitement. I had forgotten that, like Anne, I had asked to go all the way. I had asked for total transcendence, not just survival. Lulled by the peace and joy of the past four years, I was deaf to the distant rumble of thunder.

Tools to Help You
Be the Best That You Are

1. Be a saint with a sense of humor.
2. Live on the Island of Today.
3. Meditate—that is, give your time, skill, energy, love, and attention to the image of what you want to be.
4. Be the best that you are.
5. Have a love affair with life.
6. Make every day a holiday.
7. Live life and love it.
8. Ask "That I may fill up with Thee." (Author's poem)
9. Each one reach one.
10. Make gratitude your attitude as if everything were gravy.
11. Make a game of everything.
12. Make every day a *holy* day.

Chapter 5

The Deeper You Dive
the Higher You Rise

In the sunlight of a new life of the spirit, you taste
what it means to get yourself out of the way and let
God act through you. You seem to roll on oiled
wheels even in little things such as finding a parking
space, packing for a trip, cleaning the house. You are,
in fact, "high" on God. You have not only survived
suffering, you have transcended it and the tyranny of
trivia. You are grateful for the bonus of answer to
prayers for others as well as yourself, and the concrete results of seeing your person-to-person rescue
work bear fruit. Even cleansing your defects goes
smoothly. You find it a challenge, not a hardship, to
strip yourself of the old habits of thought and action,
the imperfections that still hover around you.

But something suddenly happens. It can be a major
outward event such as the death of a child, or
languishing in a concentration camp, or going blind
at the peak of your powers. Or it can be an inward
cause, a depression that swoops down on you for no
apparent reason and dims the light of your awakened
vision.

Outward or inward, the return of suffering when
you thought you had finished with it forever is called
the dark night of the soul. The classic writer on this,
St. John of the Cross, a sixteenth-century Spaniard,
called his book *The Dark Night of the Soul* (Image
Books, 1959); in it he describes every facet of it, and

the distinction between the outward dark night of the senses and the inward dark night of the soul.

A modern novelist, F. Scott Fitzgerald, has also described it: ". . . In a real dark night of the soul it is always three o'clock in the morning, day after day" (*The Crack-Up*, edited by Edmund Wilson, A New Directions Book, 1945).

It can also be described as I phrased it in the steps of breakthrough: *We reached a turning point in which the old divided self battled with the emerging new self. Resistance to breakthrough is stubborn.*

Your reaction to this new suffering will in part determine how long a period or how short your dark night will last. Of course, you need to use every survival tool already given you. You must also, however, reach for a new tool that you have merely touched but not really used before. Meanwhile your suffering seems cruel by contrast with the taste of transcendence you have already had in your prayer-supported life. You must remember at this point that you are mounting on a spiraling journey. You are not zigzagging to peaks only to plummet to lower depths than before. What is actually happening is that you have risen to far greater heights spiritually than you ever dreamed possible. It is because of the new height that the present suffering seems to take you so very low.

Spiritually you will never fall as low as you were at the outset when you picked up your first major survival tool, prayer—unless of course, you turn away from God completely. Just hang on to the fact that you are far better off today, no matter what your suffering, because now you have an awakened prayer life, and you have the tools with which to survive and transcend whatever happens.

Now you also should be part of a prayer group that will help you. And you are or should be advanced enough in survival techniques to transform suffering into sacrifice, in the sense that you have God with you to redeem it and make it useful to others. But never underestimate the enemy. The old self wants you to forget these survival tools, wants you to regress to your former unsatisfactory ways of meeting suffering.

Sometimes the dark night is not even our own, but that of friends whom we love. But it seems like our own as we suffer with them.

In South Bend on Memorial Day weekend, 1965, I was completing the last proofreading on my text book on prayer, based on my doctoral dissertation. Despite a long telephone interruption I kept on working that Saturday night. At ten-thirty o'clock the phone rang again. Dorothy Christin's voice came over the wire:

"Our boy Paul has just been stabbed—he is dying! Can you come and pray with us—just be with us?"

I rushed over to St. Joseph's Hospital, up to the surgical floor, and found Dorothy, her husband Bob, and Father Putz seated white-faced outside the operating room.

"They are trying open heart massage!" Bob said. "The stab was in the heart—an accident! He was playing with a friend and they had a knife—in our basement. The boy stabbed him by accident! They had just seen a James Bond thriller and were copying one of the scenes in the show."

The dying thirteen-year-old had staggered out of the basement on to the street where Dorothy found him, held him, sent one child to call an ambulance, another to call a priest. The heart had already stopped on the operating table, raising the additional agony of whether Paul would suffer brain damage if he did survive.

We sat numbly in that brightly lighted room around the table. Then we began to pray. I begged God to save Paul's life, to help Bob and Dorothy and their nine other children. I also prayed at their request for the boy who had committed this terrible accidental act, and his parents. We waited for hours it seemed—for news from the operating room. Dorothy reminisced about Paul, beloved among the ten children because he was an oddball, an artistic, wild, lovable, interesting child. Bob was utterly shaken, his handsome face white, his hands trembling as he lit one cigarette after another. Father Putz, solid in strength and faith, tried to keep them talking. I could give no words of my own, only those the Lord gave me. We sent each other out in relays for fresh coffee from the vending machine, more cigarettes, water. Finally at two A.M. the surgeon came out, still in his splattered white gown. He said to the Christins:

"No use your staying here—you should get some rest. We have done all we can; only the hours will tell if he'll make it."

Their other children waiting at home needed them more than Paul did in his unconscious fight for life.

At ten o'clock the next morning, Dorothy called.

"He's gone. Can you come?"

I drove out to their home. Dorothy put her arms around me and cried as I walked in. Bob hugged me. Dorothy's first words were: "I feel so bad for the parents of the boy who did it. I must go and see them."

Neighbors started streaming in with coffee urns and platters of meat and sandwiches. The small house was jammed with their friends. A nun at Notre Dame where Bob taught, hearing of their loss, hitchhiked a ride the seven miles to their home and said: "Everyone out of the kitchen—this is my department." She never left it for the next three days except to go back to the convent to sleep.

I tried to console the two older brothers, Bob and George, especially George, seventeen years old, who seemed stunned with grief. He and I sat on the swing on the verandah and talked of Paul. Then we drove out to get milk shakes that I knew from experience are about the only food people in shock and grief can get down.

From then until three days later I spent all possible time with the family, running errands, taking Dorothy for short drives away from the house now filled with relatives in from Ohio, Pennsylvania, and other states for the funeral. Several thousand friends, colleagues, and students attended the funeral conducted by five priests. Living through that dark night with the Christins deepened our bond of friendship that had begun on a lighthearted plane of folk-song parties at their house, movie-going when we had had time, joking and laughing at Bob's uproarious monologues.

Now I was impressed by the magnificent behavior of these two in the face of the worst that can happen to parents; their concern for the boy who had done it, their gratitude to others for little comforts and aids. I felt privileged to share their grief with them. I carried it inside myself for months, praying all the while that they would soon recover and that something could dull the edge of their pain. They prayed literally without ceasing during the crisis. I begged God to help them find a whole new life preferably away from the scene of the tragedy.

The Christins survived and later transcended their grief. They had already attained a high place in their spiritual journey before the blow struck. They had reached that stage, so rare, where they could think of others' sufferings even in the midst of their own. Instead of self-pity, bitterness, recriminations, loss of faith, they practiced love-in-action toward the boy who did it.

Three months after Paul's death, Bob called me excitedly. He had received a wonderful offer in Washington to consult on "Upward Bound" and other educational projects for the teenage poor. Soon the whole family moved to Washington and began a totally new kind of life, stimulating in a different sense, in the great capital. Later Bob would be named president of St. Norbert's College in Wisconsin. Even a year after Paul's death, when Dorothy and Bob visited me in Florida, their native resilience, based on joy, the fruit of the spirit, kept their eyes forward not back. They had refused to make a career out of their tragedy. Instead they were giving their time and love and attention to the living, especially their own children, and the disadvantaged children of America, as a kind of memorial to Paul. Bob's marvelous sense of humor had come back and once more we shared our laughter. But we also shared occasional moments when they and I would remember just one year earlier.

Then our positions were almost reversed as the thunder rumbled louder above my head in the mounting crescendo of my battle against deportation. In Holy Week, 1966, the bill before Congress that had been protecting me since 1961 was unexpectedly threatened with defeat by the new chairman of the House immigration subcommittee who had succeeded the late Congressman Walter. The bill was saved for the time being by the strong intervention of my new sponsor, Congressman John Brademas. But the shock and fear of the weeks before that saving action had been upsetting, as I realized how very precarious my hold was on life in America. The Christins helped me enormously through our sharing and praying together. But when they left and college closed, I was still pretty shot.

I took out an old safety valve that had helped me before in crisis. *Pamper yourself* when no one else is doing so. I made myself take off to go down to my beloved Keys. I even stopped on the way to do something I had never allowed myself to do before. I went to watch the porpoises perform at Santini's in Marathon. Just gazing at their powerful, graceful dives and leaps restored joy to my soul. And then I began to notice that Mitzie, the star porpoise of the show, said to be Flipper's one-time star, got the momentum for her superb dives by plunging to the very depths of the water. Next the sentence floated to mind:

"The deeper I dive, the higher I rise."

I meditated on that joyful picture of Mitzie diving deep, then soaring skyward, for the next months. It meant to me that the plunge I had just taken to the depth of fear when the bill had almost died, could be a springboard propelling me to a higher leap than ever before. As always I shared this thought and

97

sentence in a talk I gave at a retreat in Michigan. I urged one man in particular, who came to me for prayer, to ponder this sentence and pray it for his own survival. Months later at a low dip in my spiral way, the sentence returned to me. The postman brought it wrapped in a brown paper package. I took out a burlap banner glowing with orange, red, blue, and green letters pasted around a porpoise diving into waves and a dove flying upward. The letters spelled out:

The deeper I dive, the higher I rise.

Attached to the banner was a note from the man for whom I had prayed. He said:

> Here is the long promised wall hanging. I made it out of gratitude—because this one sentence has saved my life. I clung to it all through the months that I was told I had terminal cancer. I prayed it and other prayers constantly. But I think it was this sentence that helped me survive. It worked. God worked. The doctor now says that the original diagnosis of cancer was wrong. I am well and working at a job I love.

The sentence also helped Anne, the English nurse. I sent it to her in a letter to England in response to her plea for prayer. Anne met her dark night of the senses on a summer visit home. A doctor friend, noticing her loss of weight, insisted upon more explicit tests than she had been given in America. He told her the grim findings: tuberculosis, so advanced that her right lung would have to be removed. Though her active world ended with his words, she prayed and asked me to pray that at least her lung would be saved. Our prayer groups in Florida and Indiana and Chicago joined in praying for her.

One month later another letter came from England. A new specialist said that surgery was not necessary. Some miraculous progress had taken place in the lung. Though she must stay in bed for nearly a year, she was on the mend.

When she returned to America, Anne told me, "I could almost feel the prayers of all of you. I knew I had to keep my mind mobile even though my body was immobile. I doubled my Scripture reading. I practiced meditation for longer hours than ever. I even began teaching myself French and Italian, so that I would keep my mind growing. But my main survival came through prayer and of course the Sacraments."

Though her physical dark night had ended, her interior dark night had just begun. Unable to return to the strenuous life of the wards, she went through a distressing year of readjustment. She couldn't find just the right type of office nursing. She also suffered with a friend whose cataract surgery she voluntarily nursed. But the Lord seemed very far away. He seemed not to answer any of her prayers. She was not only plagued by threats of a relapse, but her best friends moved far away. She felt utterly alone, trying to surrender to the God whom she couldn't feel, hear, or see. Then slowly, very slowly, the light began to flicker on. She began to sense the presence of God again. She found a far less exhausting job at a clinic with other nurses.

Anne could no longer perform any physical labor for her friends, but she could and did do little things for them—send them notes, call them, pray for them, encourage them. She rejoiced when she began to see changes in their lives while her own life became integrated, balanced among her prayer, work, and study. She had emerged as a true nurse, maternally oriented toward the world, not just her family and friends. She practiced *heal others to heal yourself;* the more she prayed for others to be healed, the better her own health became. Today she shows those "high spirits peculiar to high spirituality," called by Evelyn Underhill the mark of those who have attained the unitive state.

It is a joy to be with Anne, as I was during a difficult time in Chicago doing some television stints. Interviews that would have been a strain on me, because of my cold bordering on flu, became lightened by laughs interspersed with prayer. Anne's joy in living is based not only on her complete emergence from both dark nights of the senses and of the soul, but on her selfless delight in God and his actions.

I found this quality of joy when I had lunch with John Howard Griffin and his family a few years ago in Fort Worth, Texas. Tall, white-faced, frail, John survived one of the longest dark nights of the senses I have encountered. If he could be filled with joy despite his sufferings, then it makes me feel rather shabby not to try to emulate him. John's best known work is *Black Like Me* (Houghton Mifflin, 1961), the book that did as much to launch the 1960s civil rights movement as had Harriet Beecher Stowe's *Uncle Tom's Cabin* a century earlier.

Others have survived more intensive short-term suffering in wars, prison camps, in the underground forces during World War II. But John's dark night began in and continued long after World War II. Wounded in an explosion in the South Pacific, he lay unconscious for three days until rescued. When he regained consciousness, the promising young musician, writer, and photographer, who needed his eyes for each of his great talents, was told he faced total blindness.

For twelve years he tried to transcend his blindness, even learning how to type from a special teacher of the blind. Once armed with this skill he sat down and wrote his magnificent novel in seven weeks, *The Devil Rides Outside* (Pocket Books, 1964). The war took a further toll. He became paralyzed from the hips down—the result of a malaria bug lodged in his spine during the war. He was put on a treatment of drugs to cure the paralysis and the malaria. By one of those miracles, not only did he walk again, but his vision returned.

During his blindness and paralysis John continued his creative work of writing. Now he could return to his teaching of music and his beloved photography. That should be a full enough life for any man, especially since he had married a lovely music student of his, Piedy, and begun raising his family of four.

But John, a white Texan, was not content to express himself creatively as husband, father, writer, photographer, musicologist. He was surrounded by men, women, and children whose skin color barred them from any such full self-expression, and even from rudimentary education in the segregated schools. The artist turned man of action and reporter. He decided to write about the plight of his black brothers not from the outside, from a white skin, but from inside a black skin. He got a doctor to inject him with chemicals to blacken his fair complexion so he could more easily pass as a black man. He lived and was accepted as a black in the South. The rest is history. The paperback edition of *Black Like Me* sold millions, spreading like wild fire, and like fire it touched off the mass support that led to the civil rights movement and demonstrations at Selma and Montgomery and throughout the South, and finally forced Congress to enact the civil rights laws—long overdue—implementing the hundred-year-old Fourteenth and Fifteenth Amendments. A start was made in reparations toward the black people of America.

John's price for this work was further physical suffering. He was not only stripped to the bone, he was stripped of bone. The injections that made him black destroyed his jaw bone. Many painful operations finally built him a new jaw out of ground calf bone. Each tooth had to be planted in that tissue as you would hammer a piece of timber into a post hole. He had to undergo so much surgery that he said: "When the doctor tells me he wants me back in the hospital on Wednesday, I don't even ask him why or for how long."

John's output, far from ceasing during these painful operations, continued in books, portraits, and photographic journalism. He had to learn how to talk again since his jaw was rebuilt, and was soon back lecturing, when not writing or taking pictures.

"I always explain about my rebuilt jaw when I give a talk," he said. "That way the audience doesn't give all its attention to wondering about my strange way of speaking and can pay attention to what I am saying."

Actually he sounded fine. When I first heard his

voice on the phone I thought he had a Scots accent. But he told me it was the way the speech therapist told him to handle his calf-bone jaw.

Aside from that comment and the one about not knowing what to expect when ordered to hospital, John never mentioned any of his illnesses, accidents, wounds of battle. It was his wife Piedy who answered all my questions about his physical survival. I wanted to get that picture first before meeting him as she drove me to their home. And, as she said, some of the surgery and results have been written up in medical journals. John himself was so free from self-occupation that I forgot his medical history while being with him.

"I have the writer's disease. I only live at the typewriter. I am happiest there."

Yet in the next breath he scoffed at those "writers" who tell their wives and families that writing comes first. He said they are fools and not usually writers at all. John, I observed, put his family first. They have one of those casual love affairs with each other which is delightful to behold in our age. John himself, standing at the stove in a long, faded blue, man's apron, had been preparing a delicious lunch for all of us, when I arrived with Piedy. He was a family man to the core. But he was also an artist, the solitary man that an artist must be. He turned solitary once a month when he went for ten days to the Trappist monastery, Gethsemane, in Kentucky to work on the private diaries of the late Father Louis, Trappist priest, known to the world as Thomas Merton, author of *The Seven Storey Mountain* (Harcourt, Brace & World, 1948)) and dozens of other works. These diaries were so well guarded that they could not be photostated or removed from Gethsemane.

The Trappist abbot, to make John's research easier, used some of Tom's royalties, which he earned for the monastery, to fit out Tom's hermitage for the invalid John, complete with a hospital bed so that John could work in bed when ailing. The abbot also lent him the electric typewriter Tom used. John followed the Trappist rule, rising at three A.M. and going to bed at eight P.M. when spending his ten days each month. He saw no human being until six o'clock at night when two Trappist priests came over to the hermitage, celebrated the Lord's Supper, the Mass, and John cooked them a real treat, meat, for dinner. This was the only time the Trappists got meat.

One day John was sitting at Tom's typewriter, reading and taking notes on Tom's diaries, his last days before he suffered his freak accident. Tom was in Bangkok for a conference on the future of monastic life in Asia, following pilgrimages to leading Eastern mystics, mainly Buddhist, whom he had long admired. He turned on the electric fan in his room. He was electrocuted instantly.

John, sitting at Tom's typewriter, was happy as he always is at the task of writing. But as his fingers touched the keys, he was struck by a bolt of lightning. He lay near death for days. Even when he regained consciousness he had no idea who he was. The abbot said they feared his brain had been "sizzled" to a crisp. Doctors told him that the lightning had pierced his pancreas, destroying its production of insulin.

The abbot said drily, "John seems to suffer the same experiences he writes about." Just as he was writing about Tom's death by electric shock, he himself was struck by lightning in Tom's own chair, within Tom's own hermitage.

War had blinded John and paralyzed him; dedication to civil rights had stripped his face of bone. Dedication to the memory of his friend Tom nearly cost him his mind and his life. For though the brain recovered, the pancreas never did, leaving him an incurable diabetic. Eventually the oral insulin stopped its effectiveness in treatment. A painful right leg, more visits to the hospital, and shots of insulin followed. But for the writer, the worst was, according to him:

"They gave me so much pain-killing stuff that my mind became too blurred to work for three months. I am just getting back to work now—going up to Gethsemane tomorrow to get back to the Merton book."

How did John Howard Griffin not only survive but transcend all these physical vicissitudes for more than thirty-five years? First of all, he minimized them, saying, "My only suffering has been physical." But his fuller answer to transcending suffering was given in a major piece on the subject, called "The Terrain of Physical Pain," with other articles in a book called *Creative Suffering*, (Alan Paton, et al., The National Catholic Reporter with Pilgrim Press, 1970). Though John wrote in the third person, the reader knows it is from the depth of his own unchosen vocation of suffering that he was able to help others. He used none of the clichés sometimes offered by pietistic friends, for example:

Nothing is more ironic to the man steeped in physical pain than to be told by the visitor, pink-cheeked with health, that the sufferer is "God's pet," or that God has allowed him "the deep privilege of suffering," even though these things may have some truth in them.

But John did not attempt to escape awareness of his pain. He, like his late friend, the French poet Raissa Maritain, developed the faculty of transcending it on two planes—"that of concrete experience, demanding and painful, and that of an abstract and liberating conception rooted in the same experience."

John interprets it this way:

This faculty to act at once on two planes can be dissipated when it becomes merely an attempt to escape an awareness of pain. No, it must be the contrary, an acceptance and an awareness of the reality that exists in pain and that sometimes becomes obsessive in pain, and then a growing ability, from the same root, to stand off and become the observer; and then again, passing on to the observation of other things until at length and in the natural order of things, the observing self comes to the realization that self, even in pain, is less interesting than other objects of contemplation. It is this realization, which takes time, that ultimately liberates the sufferer: not from his suffering, no; not from an acute awareness of his suffering, no; but from the otherwise exclusive, obsessive, paralyzing, sterilizing enslavement of suffering.

The liberation comes also from the fact that the sufferer is "reawakened to mercy and to that whole mysterious cycle of replenishment in which he has allowed himself to be used, to be an instrument, a filter."

John quoted Father Gerald Vann, the Dominican, from his work *The Divine Pity* (Doubleday, Image paperback, 1961), when he says, "The merciful shall obtain more than they can desire. How is that? Because pity enlarges the heart, and where there is infinite pity, there is infinite enlargement of the heart, and so an infinite capacity for joy—and what joy is, no man can tell. . . ."

John died September 8, 1980, at the age of sixty. "Piedy, his widow, said, 'John died of *everything*,' " wrote Robert Ellsberg, associate editor of the *Catholic Worker*, in the December, 1980 issue of the newspaper. Ellsberg went on: "He suffered from virtually every affliction under the sun: diabetes, bad kidneys, emphysema, a weak heart. . .skin cancer, one product of the treatments he had endured so long ago."

Long before I met John, a few brief letters from him helped me more than any words from any human being during my own dark night, not of the senses, but of the soul. That dark night broke like a sudden storm on a bright sunny day in May, 1967. I was sitting at the typewriter rejoicing that I had the whole summer free of teaching and might even finish my book. I was staying with friends in Miami for a week. The phone interrupted my writing. The call was from Washington. It was the assistant to Congressman Brademas, the new sponsor of my private bill in Congress. Her voice was high pitched, as she asked:

"Dr. Anthony, are you sitting down? I am afraid I have bad news for you. The committee has killed your bill! You will be deported in less than thirty days!"

They gave no reason, she said. They didn't have to.

The killing of the bill meant that I must get ready right now to leave America, never to return. Congress could do nothing more for me. I must report immediately to the immigration director in Miami.

Though numb with shock, I automatically shifted gears into my emergency survival procedure. First, I typed a prayer for help, which then became *a list of what I had to do to survive*, beginning with my call to the immigration director. Then I made myself coffee to remind myself to stay away from a drink. Later I forced myself to eat, even when the immigration director said he could do nothing for me unless I tried to prove I was an *anti*-left wing as I had once been *pro*-left wing. This was tantamount to telling me my case was hopeless.

Throughout the night-and-day battle to win a stay of deportation, helped by two lawyers, I tried to keep a steady hand, and was forced to keep at the typewriter. Now I typed not my book, but the scores of facts the lawyers needed for their brief. I used every tool I had been given in my survival kit to keep going *one day at a time*. But when those days dwindled down to only ten, I had to fight against tears, against total collapse. Then I was saved by my long time tools of *each one reach one, heal others to heal yourself*.

I was given the care of a nineteen-year-old girl, Fran. She dreaded not the pain of giving birth to her illegitimate baby, but the pain of parting with it. She must, she had been told, place him for adoption. We became prayer partners. Daily I prayed for her safe delivery in the hospital. Daily she prayed for my safe deliverance from deportation. Her actual confinement took place on the very day I was taken to immigration authorities to learn my fate. My lawyers and I walked into the grim fortress-like building in downtown Miami. The district director announced the good news that immigration *would* not only give me a stay of deportation, but he promised an immediate new hearing on my case.

Filled with joy at my temporary deliverance, I rushed to call Fran. She had just delivered her baby boy. We both quickly forgot our agonies. My hope now was that I would emerge from my seven years of nationality limbo. I celebrated during the next twenty-four hours by calling the news of the hearing, the stay of deportation, to my brother and sisters, friends and sponsors. It wasn't until nine o'clock that night that my lawyer could get through on the busy phone. He said:

"Susan, you won't like it—but there's not a thing we can do. Immigration has postponed—indefinitely —any new hearing on your case."

It was like running up to win at the finish line, but stumbling inches before the tape. For the first time in the three weeks' struggle, I did break into tears. I then sought the only solace I knew, a walk on the beach to try to get quiet and reach my Lord. But he seemed dead in His tomb, as I was dead in mine. Was this then the dark night of the soul, the death of God in my life?

Like a battle-fatigued veteran, I dragged myself north to my annual prayer conference at Notre Dame, Indiana. A virus mowed me down physically for months. I tried to hide my exhaustion from Mother when I visited her in Pennsylvania. Maternally intuitive, she kept asking me what was the matter. We had tried to keep the deportation crisis from her. I simply could not break it to her that one day soon she and I might be saying a final farewell on this earth. With heavy heart and weakened body I started the tedious solitary drive from Pennsylvania back to college in Florida. I tried all the way down to pump life into my drooping spirit by repeating, "The deeper I dive, the higher I rise." But nothing happened. I looked unseeing at the survival symbol I had carried with me all summer on the seat beside me in the car. It was a heavy lead cross, crowned with a glowing bronze dove superimposed on it. The dove's head, body, and wings all but hid the cross symbolizing to me, *the spirit does transcend the cross.*

Jesus not only died for us but He rose and He lives for us. He sent the Holy Spirit to comfort us and teach us to transcend. My mind accepted this but it was still three o'clock in the morning in my dark night of the soul.

I was speeding down the Florida turnpike at a dangerous pace, dreading my return to college. I passed a herd of drought-parched cattle searching for a blade of grass in the baked, brown earth, their dappled hides stretched tight over the protruding skeletons of hip bones. Their mute misery in the white hot sun brought two lines from the Holy Spirit:

World that I love my heart aches for you—
World that I love my heart breaks for you.

Hot tears burned and I drove along drenched in pity for the suffering of all beasts and children and adults. I became overwhelmed with a sense of oneness with all suffering life, a sense of infinite pity. This pity was rooted in the needs of others, seeking to act for others, to strengthen and build them up. It was a redemptive pity. And it began to enlarge my heart and even open it up to a bit of strange joy. "World that I love my heart aches for you" began to stir in me a desire to redeem the suffering of the world about me. I began to see that my girlhood efforts to change the world, my youthful activism for pacifism, feminism, civil rights, and antifascism, had sought the right goals, but had been rooted in the wrong motives. I had been lacking in the quality of redemptive pity. As Father Vann says, ". . .You can only redeem and restore [the world] in the degree to which being first redeemed and restored yourself, you have learned to love."

In that autumn of 1967 I began to identify not only with the suffering individual, but once again with the victims of war and poverty and injustice, the wholesale planetary sufferers. And I learned that *my* suffering had become less interesting than that of others, as John Howard Griffin had learned. I would try to make my suffering redemptive and usable for others—no more passive, flattened out exhaustion, or, on the other hand, resentful rebellion.

Someone arrived to guide me in these first steps, a survivor of the largest scale suffering inflicted by man upon man in our history, the Nazi extermination camps. His name was Rabbi Isaac Neuman. He arrived on campus within the month of my return. Lighthearted and cheerful, he lifted us up with his scholarly yet fascinating lectures on Hebrew scripture. He was a witness of love and joy and peace.

I needed what he had, so I invited him to come to the beach with me for a swim and a talk. I wanted to find the source of his spiritual and psychological survival and transcendence. How had he survived so

well the Nazi death camp Auschwitz and the extermination of his family? As we walked on the beach
together, he told me:

> I survived because my suffering was meaning-
> ful—I refused to become an animal. Today I talk
> about it. I do not let it build up inside—I share
> what happened to me, not only to help others
> but to help myself. Why aren't you doing the
> same? Why aren't you telling your story, getting
> it out of your system? You recovered from
> alcoholism by sharing it. You can recover from
> your years of captivity by talking and writing
> about it.

That night he spoke to a large audience on campus.
As he finished, the first question came from a
Catholic priest: "What did you say your brand
number was, Rabbi?"
Isaac told him. The priest took off his jacket, rolled
up a sleeve, and walked to the stage. Isaac walked
down the steps to meet him. The Jewish rabbi and the
Roman Catholic priest embraced each other. They
had both been imprisoned at Auschwitz, the Polish
priest because of his nationality, the rabbi because of
his religion.
I couldn't follow Isaac's advice to speak in public
about my deportation crisis, so minor compared with
his experience. My lawyers had warned me not to
state anything in public. It might jeopardize my case.
But nothing stopped me from writing about it. The
action of writing proved a great catharsis while I was
waiting for the verdict of the immigration officials. It
was part of the help I received as the months became a
year.

The Deeper You Dive the Higher You Rise

The dove on the cross now hung above my type-writer where I glanced at it whenever I looked up. The Spirit it symbolized seemed to be beckoning me to a further yielding, a further surrender to Him— one that would rid me of the tension of waiting, worrying, resisting. I began to pray for this further surrender, and for the power of the charismatic gifts that the Spirit gives, even more gifts than those He had already given me, in prayer and action for others.

One night while I was walking on the beach in prayer, He answered by giving me the gift of praising God—not in the poems of earlier years, not even in any language that I could understand. He gave me the gift of tongues, the ancient apostolic method of praising the Lord in an unknown language, called glossolalia. This childlike gift was a welcome rest to me, because I spend most of my days searching for words to match my thoughts. Now I could sing and speak in this unknown tongue, knowing that the Holy Spirit was praying and praising in me. The event, called the Baptism in the Holy Spirit, seemed to give me added strength to turn away from my own problem and launch more prayer groups. He rewarded me by giving me what I had long prayed for, a prayer community. A few weeks after I received that in-filling of the Holy Spirit, the gift of tongues marking it, I went to my new class of students at Marymount for its first meeting. Sitting there were a dozen adult women from nearby towns in South Florida. They became the core of our community. They helped put on prayer group leaders' workshops. They founded their own prayer groups. They taught prayer at Sunday school and in church. They did not run frightened even when each of them received a poison pen letter from a local extreme right-wing group attacking me as a one-time Red. The prayer community helped me survive fully as much as I taught them about prayer.

But back in my little cottage, alone, I would find myself listing which books I would give away if I lost my battle against exile. Though I tried to discount this behavior as negative, I kept returning to it, even writing down to whom I would bequeath my few possessions—my stereo, portable television, and the two Empire gilt mirrors and brass student lamps my father had given me. I kept that list in case the federal marshal came to my door to force me onto the deportation plane trip.

I had traveled light all these years in citizenship limbo so I had little to ditch; I would take my clothes and my typewriter with me. But I would also carry the one prized possession—that weighed nothing, that could not be scrutinized by customs officials. It was invisible and was built right into the heart of me. It was my survival kit. Midway in that dark wood of waiting for the immigration hearing, the Holy Spirit gave me a prayer poem that not only consoled me but directed me to what I knew I now must do.

> The century is my home
> Not nation, state or town.
> My native land I love
> But it's no longer mine
> To call my home.
>
> The century is my home—
> A home not bound by space
> Nor fixed in place—but time
> You've given me
> To call my home.

The Deeper You Dive the Higher You Rise

The century is my home
Until that day You lift me from all time
And let me make my home with You,
In my true patria
The everlasting country of the soul.

For I'm a citizen of the century
This century You've given to me.
This century of nuclear warheads
Of crashed banks, barbed wire and bombs.
I'm a citizen of this century
Of love and destruction of love.

Let me sing the beloved century
Sustain me in this my love song
Of kinship with those in my century
The kinship whose suffering I share.

Of kinship with those in all centuries—
Premature pilgrims who dare
To leap ahead of their centuries
In their thought, their deed and their prayer—

Prayer to You that this century
Will march on to its journey's end
Not down to the ape and the darkness
But up to the kinship of men.

Tools to Help You Survive
the Dark Night of the Soul

1. You'll reach a turning point in which the old divided self battles with the emerging new self. Resistance to breakthrough is stubborn.
2. Pamper yourself.
3. Pray without ceasing.
4. The deeper you dive, the higher you rise.
5. Heal others to heal yourself.
6. Write down your survival schedule each night. Cross off each accomplishment at the end of the day.
7. The spirit transcends the cross.
8. "World that I love my heart aches for you—
World that I love my heart breaks for you." (Author's poem)

Chapter 6

Will to Will the Will of God

Survival kit tools only help you if you *remember to remember* to pick them up and use them. The major tool of surrender I had used when I began my recovery from alcoholism in 1946. But I had not made a total surrender of the rest of my life. It was similar to my experience in using the cleansing tools for the main defect of alcoholism, but I had left the rest of my defects intact, until involuntarily I was purged and stripped.

When the Lord gave me the poem, "The Century Is My Home," it showed my compliance, but certainly not my surrender to the possibility of lifetime exile from America. And there is a difference. Compliance is skin-deep, surface surrender, halfhearted and grudging. Surrender is a deep interior yielding, an acceptance of the will of God. He had given me the words for it but not the will to will it in that first prayer-poem years earlier.

> And whatever may happen to me,
> I say, Blessed be the name of Thee.

Even earlier He had given me the words of the late theologian Reinhold Niebuhr:

> God grant me the serenity
> To accept the things I cannot change
> Courage to change the things I can
> And wisdom to know the difference.

Now He began to show me what a surrendered person was like in the flesh. One of the first was the English healing minister, Brother Mandus—one of the happiest men I have ever met. He attributes his joy to the unconditional surrender he made on an ordinary day at home. He had been walking from the kitchen to the dining room where he was helping dry the dishes and put them away. In that short walk the Lord told Brother Mandus to hand over his life to Him and directed him to read John 15:16:

> You did not choose me, but I chose you and appointed you that you should go and bear fruit and that your fruit should abide; so that whatever you ask the Father in my name he may give it to you.

This meant to Brother Mandus that he must start praying to heal others. From small beginnings right where he lived, in Blackpool, England, he began an apostolate that today reaches millions of people in the World Healing Crusade, through talks, on tape, in books, pamphlets, and his magazines. When I met him, I asked him to pray that I too might make an unconditional, lifetime surrender. He did. I immediately began practicing the prayer Jesus said at Gethsemane, ". . .not my will but Thine be done" (Luke 22:42). But I added to it as Brother Mandus suggested, "Thy will for me is perfect everything." The miracle of surrender did not take place, since I was trying to run the show by asking for perfect *outward* conditions.

Just a month before my encounter with Jesus, I met another surrendered soul in the flesh. He was Thomas Powers, author of *First Questions on the Life of the Spirit* (Harper, 1959). I journeyed out to his home in suburban New York (several years before he founded his unique community for helping alcoholics recover, East Ridge.) Tom was a slim man in his forties who looked like a lighthearted leprechaun, despite the lines of suffering marking his cheeks. His pale eyes had the unclouded gaze of the mystic. The richness of his voice, added to the words he said, held me entranced for three hours in his garden. Tom said he too had tried for years to make a total surrender of his will and his life to God. He had been as unsuccessful as I. Then the day came when he was hit by one of the worst crises of his life. It involved not only his marriage, his family, but his whole physical and emotional nature. He plummeted into the dark night during which even his mind was dulled and his generally fluent tongue inarticulate, at a time when he needed all his faculties. He couldn't even read. Then he was led to a book he had earlier rejected. Now he could read nothing but this book, and he read none other during the months of his crisis. As he wrote in *First Questions:*

> Never, never before had I even half realized the power of a holy man of God to reach out over the centuries and across the oceans and to give to a modern man, so far separated from him in the flesh, his blessing of living knowledge, living courage, living love.

This holy man was Father Jean Pierre de Caussade, a Jesuit priest living in obscurity in France from 1675 to 1751, serving as spiritual director to some Sisters of the Visitation. It was his letters of direction, introduction, and commentary that took shape in today's edition of his masterpiece, *Self-Abandonment to Divine*

Providence (Templegate, 1963). In this book Tom found the message that he passed on to his readers and to me in person.

Surrender this present moment; practice the "sacrament of the present moment." It is not necessary to surrender tomorrow or next year, but just this moment. Nor is it necessary to know the will of God for tomorrow. It is only necessary to accept, to abandon yourself to God's will as it unfolds in your life *moment to moment*. Surrender this present moment to God since at this moment, this is God's will for you. Whether it is a letter of rejection, the diagnosis of an illness, the loss of a job, a triumph, or suffering, what this moment brings is God's will for you.

Sufficient unto the *moment* is the suffering or joy thereof. Do not try to anticipate God's will for you tomorrow, or next year. Simply accept as God's present intention for you, what happens at this particular moment. It was no coincidence that I was trying to practice this sacrament of the present moment, when Jesus became God in my life. Nor was it coincidence that He sent me one of the greatest examples of surrender to help me on my way, immediately after my conversion to Jesus.

It was during those winter months of 1961 that I met Mme. Induk Pahk whose prayers, as I have mentioned, directed me to get Congressional protection through the private bill. But she did far more than that. She presented herself to me as a living portrait in my gallery of surrendered souls. Nor had she come to her surrender easily, as she told me, and also her readers in her fine book, *The Hour of the Tiger* (Harper & Row, 1965).

For years Induk had slaved to earn pennies,

quarters, and dollars by speaking all over the United State to finance her dreamed of Berea-in-Korea craft school for South Korean children. The time came when she had amassed three thousand dollars and put it in a savings bank. An old friend, whom she had known in Korea, called her up and told her a wonderful way to double her interest. He would, he said, invest her money and put it to work for her. She had no reason to suspect him of anything but good intentions. She handed over to him the entire amount of her precious savings, three thousand dollars.

For a time she received interest in cash. Then she stopped receiving anything at all from him. She called him up to be told by him that he had invested his money and hers into the building business. He promised that they'd both be earning 15 percent. Though she thought this high, she was told it was an American custom. She continued her transcontinental journeys, lecturing to raise money, and sent every penny she earned to this same "investor."

One day she was with her daughter, Iris, at home in Washington. A bailiff appeared at the door. He served Induk with a summons to appear in court on charges of usury. Stunned and baffled, she saw her dreams collapse, her life work finished. Her daughter studied the summons. She immediately saw through it. The "investor," fearing that Induk might sue him for loss of her money, took the offensive and sued her first.

She did not close her eyes that night, nor for many sleepless nights after this blow. Though she tried to keep up with her already arranged lectures, she gave them in a daze. Over and over again she rehearsed the incident that had shattered her and her dreams for her school. Audiences were now turned off instead of turned on by her spiritless talks. Her invitations dwindled. She was at the bottom.

Frantically she accepted an invitation to go on retreat at the Episcopalian Conference Center in Massachusetts. She clutched at the retreat as her last chance to try to rid herself of her burden of hate and hurt. For seven days and nights she prayed to be delivered of it. Nothing happened. The betrayal still festered in her.

On the last night of the retreat she forlornly went to her special refuge, a quiet chapel in the big, old retreat house. In her book she describes in her own words what happened. She heard "the soft deep chiming of a clock striking the hour of midnight—each note slow and separate and silver. And as the last note struck twelve, out of nowhere came the word—softly, softly, in the sleepy voice of a railroad conductor— 'Kyoto! Kyoto!' "

That word would mean nothing to many Americans, but to Induk on her knees in Massachusetts, it instantly recalled the magic city, Kyoto, in Japan. Years earlier, before World War II, she had boarded a train for Yokohama to set sail for the United States for a new life after a severe crisis. Half dozing in the coach she had heard the conductor call out, "Kyoto! Kyoto!" It was exactly midnight as she heard the conductor's voice fade away. She sat upright in her seat. "Midnight! The dividing point." The dark night had ended. The new day was reaching toward dawn, toward light. She had put her suffering behind her at that moment, and begun her new life.

Now, a quarter of a century later and thousands of miles across the world, in a little chapel in New

England, the chimes of midnight once more marked a turning point, between the darkest night and the light. She rose from her knees, liberated of her resentment. She had let go, left the hurt in the chapel. She had been given the grace of surrender, a surrender that gives peace, not as the world gives it, but as Jesus gives it.

She had found that *the road to transcending is through surrendering,* and out of that revelation came the survival sentence, "I will to will the will of God," that she later passed on to me when I needed it.

From then on she let God lead. When she spoke a few days later to a group of women in a church, she felt the power of her new surrender. Now the audience was enthusiastic. Now as she wrote in *The Hour of the Tiger,* "I felt within me the wellsprings of a new power."

Nor was that just a one-shot experience. The new Induk Pahk was a new and powerful speaker. She no longer set a fixed fee for her talks, but trusted the Lord and her audiences for a voluntary offering. A church in Florida gave her more than she had ever received, $580. She journeyed faster and faster from one speech to another, relying completely on the openhandedness of her audiences. Whereas once she received only a few dollars for a talk, now she earned several hundred dollars every time she mounted the platform. Even her mailbox in Washington began to fill up with gift checks sent by friends for the school fund. The savings account, which had been totally wiped out, began to grow like mushrooms in a forest.

Her total surrender turned to triumph. Five years later she could write, "I have arrived at my destination after travelling so far for so long."

Berea-in-Korea, the school for boys, became a reality on March 20, 1964, in Seoul, Korea, a living testimony to Induk Pahk's surrender and to her faith and hard work of thirty-five years. She told me when she visited my class in Florida that had she not made that total surrender on that May midnight, all would have been lost. Never could she have picked up the pieces of her life and attained the victory.

I journeyed to meet another surrendered soul out in the desert in California. He was one of the most dramatic converts in our century. Starr Daily, when I met him, certainly did not look like a hardened, troubled criminal. He was tall, white-haired, almost saintly looking. Yet he had spent a large part of his life behind bars, justly. There he had broken most of the penitentiary rules in his rebellion against all authority. He was sent into solitary confinement repeatedly. He refused to listen to his one friend in prison, an old man, a "lifer," who begged him to try another way, the way of Christ. Starr went from bad to worse. His periods in solitary stretched for longer and longer durations. One day, in his rat-infested solitary cell, the Lord came to him. He asked Starr for his surrender, for his complete life. Starr replied, "Yes."

From that day on he became a model prisoner, began studying the Scriptures, applied for parole, and began learning to write. He also found a pen-pal, the lady who later became his wife. His great book, *Love Can Open Prison Doors* (Willing Pub. Co., 1934), tells this story climaxed by his release from prison. Later books cover his amazing mission converting thousands of people by his talks, books, and later by the Camps Farthest Out, country retreats held everywhere in America, launched by Starr and Glenn Clark and Frank Laubach.

You might object that Starr, Induk Pahk, Brother Mandus, and Thomas Powers are giants of the spiritual life, that their surrender is impossible for ordinary people like you and me. But I was to watch the transformation of abandonment in our friend Martin, the one who was once the greedy executive, the poor sport college teacher, still trying to act the big shot playing the market and making real estate deals.

Martin had made real progress in his cleansing and his prayer life in the year after the crisis brought on by bulldozers and cement mixers. He had begun to show a real concern for his students, as well as his family. His greediness was transmuted into a hunger for more of God in his life. He said he wanted to go all the way with God, using all the survival and transcending tools he was learning in the group, including the sixth step of the breakthrough:

"We surrender ourselves to God, moment by moment, seeking the state of abandonment to God as a way of life."

When I returned to Florida after my usual summer trip north I called his wife Martha, who invited me to dinner. Afterward they told me of the events of the summer. Martin had let resentment come back into his life. His nemesis, another construction job right next door to their own home, had ruined July for him. Then their air conditioning system broke down and he was furious that he could not afford the expensive repairs. He fretted and fumed in the sultry August heat. Then one night, after exploding in anger, he felt chest pains. Martha called the ambulance, which carried him to the hospital. He was laid on the shiny metal table in the emergency room to wait for the doctor.

"As I lay on that cold table in that sterile little room, I knew I was very close to death," he said. "I could feel the pain in my heart, knew that I could conk out at any moment. One moment I was literally frightening myself to death. The next moment something said, 'Okay, Lord, if you want to, take me now. I've had a good life. Into your hands I commit my spirit.' "

He fell asleep in a peaceful doze and was in this relaxed state when the doctor examined him. He needed no tranquilizers, only medicine for his heart attack. His recovery amazed the doctors and the staff. Less than a month later, he looked better than I had ever seen him, trimmer from his new diet, but, more than that, he radiated a calm, benign spirit. He had let go and let God. Martin has become the kind of man whom his friends and children journey two thousand miles to visit. I know because I have met some of them, and I, too, like to be near him, hoping that some of that peace and calm will rub off. He is surrendered and free of fear. What more really could you want?

Today the menace warping the lives of many people is not the bomb, bad as it is, but personal fear, fear of disease, accident, and especially of cancer. The cancer fear is magnified by constant advertising and publicity hammering away to remind us of it a dozen times a day. We saw how Dorrie, the working wife prayer group member, handled the diagnosis of cancer, with prayer and faith, and she has passed her five-year recovery period with no trace of a recurrence.

It seemed as though Sarah Gainham had already experienced as much tragedy as one life could hold, with her overcoming of her childhood memories of her parents' murder. But one day I received a brief note from her: "Please pray and have your prayer groups pray for me. I have cancer of the uterus."

Later she told me how she survived this experience. She used all the tools and safety valves she had learned in transcending the childhood experience. But she added some more:

> The day I learned I had cancer, I went to a nursery and bought some seeds, and I am not a great gardener. I sort of enjoy it in a calm kind of way. But that was a very comforting thing to me to be planting something that I was going to watch grow while I was waiting to find out what was going to happen.

She laughed as she said, "Incidentally they didn't grow very well—but at the time it served a very good purpose."

While she was recovering her strength from the radiation treatment, she prayed constantly to transcend her fear of surgery. She tried not to think about it. She kept busy doing little things to make her home more attractive and comfortable. She did lots of physical things, even though she is not normally an enthusiastic housekeeper. But she cleaned cupboards and made the pantry over. She then went to care for her daughter's brand new baby. When she got home from being a grandmother, the doctor confirmed that she would indeed require surgery, a total hysterectomy. Always extremely apprehensive about hospitals, she dreaded this final trip. She had already made two visits, the first when she learned she had cancer; the second for radiation, three or four weeks later. Five weeks later, on the eve of surgery, she was in low spirits. Then the words came to her, "This is not Operation Day, this is Lifesaving Day." This made it look quite a bit better she said.

The words "lifesaving day" calmed her, because she realized that without surgery she did not stand a chance of survival. She described her feelings: "That long ride down that hall to the operating room, it's the most alone thing in the world, and yet on that morning I was not alone. For the first time I wasn't alone at all. Suddenly, as I took that ride, someone was with me, walking alongside that table, and you know Who it was."

A few weeks later Sarah wrote us good news. The surgery had been completely successful; not a trace of cancer was left. She went back to her job completely recovered.

Though I had been given so many examples of surrendered souls, crowned by Jesus himself, I was still holding tight the reins of my life in 1968. I simply could not live up to my own prayer, "Whatever may happen to me, Blessed be the Name of Thee."

The fifteen-month wait for a new deportation hearing came to a sudden end. We were given short notice to appear immediately in Miami, complete with lawyers' briefs, testimonials on my character, and live testimony by friends. My lawyers, Grover Cleveland Herring and Cody Fowler, and their assistants worked intensively one long weekend. We traveled to Miami and a dingy little room in the prisonlike federal building where immigration officials had granted my stay in 1967. Now we were given a day for our briefs and witnesses. We had high hopes that a recent Supreme Court decision, the *Afroyim v. Rusk* case, would give us the verdict we sought. It ruled that Congress cannot deprive a citizen of his citizenship by any law whatsoever. This threw out a nefarious McCarthy era immigration law which had barred my entry as a citizen.

Four months passed after the hearing—four months of praying, using survival tools to carry me through. But they did little good on Christmas Eve. Somehow I had determined that my Christmas present would be the news of my repatriation. But the night before Christmas no verdict came at all. I dragged myself out to midnight Mass with a heavy heart, feeling chilled in the sudden, for Florida, cold wave. Christmas day my "present" was a bout of Hong Kong flu turning into pneumonia. Now I couldn't even pray. I simply held on to a Bible that I couldn't read. I drove down to the Keys as soon as I could to convalesce before the new semester's classes began. The message reached me there. We had lost! The government not only turned down our plea but ordered me deported within ninety days.

Once more I was supported by the prayer community. Catherine Marshall, the great spiritual author, her friend and mine, Freddie Koch, and Faith Smith, a healer, prayed with me one whole afternoon. We prayed that I might surrender, as well as for divine intervention to prevent deportation. I wrote John Howard Griffin, though I had not yet met him. I wanted his advice on my own story that I had been trying to write since Rabbi Neuman had set me to putting it down. John's letter came with that light so characteristic of him, holding out a hand over the miles to comfort and edify. I carried his letter with me up to Washington. We were being given a last resort hearing during Holy Week: forty-five minutes in which to present our final appeal. I searched the faces of the men and women who sat on the Board of Immigration Appeal. What would their verdict be? As I left the hearing room, I was surrounded by reporters who broke the story of my imminent exile in wire service stories and television news that reached, alas, my mother in Easton, before I could get the news to her. I rushed up to Easton to reassure her and try to soften the blow. I did not tell her what I had been warned: should the board rule against me, I would be instantly picked up by a federal marshal and carried off to a plane before my lawyers could even get another stay of deportation.

Nor was there a thing that my lawyers could do now. And when literally scores of long-distance calls and hundreds of letters poured in as a result of the news that I was in danger of being deported, I could say nothing to the offers of "What can I do to help?" It was after one of these calls that an idea was born. Why not ask them to pray? We can't do anything else. Why not ask all these wonderful friends who had called and written to mount a massive prayer vigil throughout the country. Everything else had failed, why not try prayer?

Catherine Marshall in Florida and Father Putz in Indiana, though separated by thousands of miles and though they had never met, became the informal sponsors of the prayer vigil, suggesting the form of the vigil and the content of the letter we would send out. John Howard Griffin contributed the key sentence in the letter when he wrote me:

. . .We are praying. . .*that perhaps a little Divine Justice can creep into the courts of human justice*. . .(italics mine) tonight at Mass we are offering as our intentions that the Holy Spirit will guide those who are to judge.

John's letter gave me not only his prayer and sympathy. As I reread it, I knew that I was reading the words of a surrendered soul. He himself summed up his life simply:

"I made my surrender once. I meant it."

Catherine, Father Putz, and John were among the more than five thousand prayer partners who conducted a nationwide prayer watch on May 2, 1969. Their prayers for my repatriation took place in churches, cathedrals, homes, convents, monasteries, and even in a federal penitentiary. One federal prisoner wrote me that he had held a prayer meeting with his fellow prisoners on my behalf. He later married the prayer partner he had met by correspondence through the prayer watch, and trained as a minister when he was released from prison. College presidents, editors, reporters, archbishops, bishops, priests, and nuns continued their prayers for me after May 2, when not a word came out of Washington following the massive effort.

While the jury was out, I tried as usual to keep my work habits intact. I taught at Marymount until Commencement Day, needing extra prayer to carry me through my farewell to my students and faculty friends. Earlier in the year, after the Miami deportation hearings, I had been told not to come back to teach next year. The stripping was continuing. With no livelihood I was trying hard to get my book in shape to present to a publisher.

On the morning of June 25 I marked off the day on my desk calendar. The jury had now been out thirteen weeks. I sat at my typewriter to begin my day's stint on the book. But today the white paper rejected me. For the first time that I could remember, not a single word came out. I couldn't even write a prayer to unloose the block. I telephoned a prayer partner, Faith Smith. We went to the beach where we prayed and shared for three hours. Faith said I must promise to let go completely, to stop my own prayers for the verdict, to leave it completely to the Lord. After all, there were, she said, thousands praying for me. Let them do the praying. My job was simply to surrender.

As I drove home the words floated to mind, "Open wide my gates with thanksgiving." But what had I to be thankful for? Again the sentence came back. I was commanded to repeat it ceaselessly, whatever might happen to me. I looked it up in the Bible when I got home and found the original version of that command. It was in Psalm 100:

> Enter his gates with thanksgiving
> and his courts with praise.

Suddenly my little cottage seemed filled with the Holy Spirit. I had that day at last made my *fiat*. I had surrendered, let go. After eighteen years as a captive of the cold war, nine years as a deportee, I had finally, belatedly, put the whole problem of exile in God's hands. That night I went about His business, driving a friend who was both alcoholic and on welfare to a meeting. I took her out afterwards for a soda, later praying with her in the car. As I walked in my own door and looked about at the room I had so often itemized for exile, I praised the Lord. I no longer felt like a stateless orphan. My *fiat* had conferred upon me full citizenship rights in the "everlasting country of the soul," the Kingdom of God on earth. I read Psalm 100 again and fell into the deep untroubled sleep of total surrender.

Next morning, June 26, I went happily back to my typewriter, the words flowing, praising the Lord for this great gift, this grace of surrender. The phone rang. But it was not Washington. It was a friend who told me of the death of another friend's husband. Could I go and call on the widow? I dropped my work at the typewriter. I drove over the few miles to comfort her. She was not at home. I followed an impulse to stop at the Deerfield Beach library and do a very strange thing. I, who had hesitated to buy 1970 license tags for my car, not knowing what country I would inhabit tomorrow, now signed up for a three-year library card. Part of me mocking my act saying, "You may never get a chance to use the card." But I banished that thought with the new part of me, the surrendered self. As I opened the door of my cottage, I heard the phone ringing and rushed to pick it up. It was my lawyer's secretary, May Hart:

You have won! The Board has upheld you. Says that you never did lose your citizenship— you are American—all deportation proceedings are dropped, terminated, finished. You are free!

Stunned by joy, I called Mother in Pennsylvania to tell her the glad news. Then I typed out a prayer of thanksgiving: "Now thank we all our God." The first line of the old hymn became the first line of what would be my thank you letter to the thousands who had helped me, who had prayed for me. Then I got on the phone and began the twelve-hour expensive but joyous task of calling my sponsors who had helped me in the battle for repatriation all these years. Long after midnight I was still trying to reach them, reasoning that I had spent hundreds of dollars so often to beg their help, to tell them bad news, that surely I could spend half that to tell them the good news and to thank them. They and I knew that our concerted prayer had accomplished in eight weeks what hard and skilled work had not done in nine years. But inwardly I knew another truth. My own final *fiat* on the verdict had opened the way for divine justice in less than twenty-four hours.

Too excited by the taste of unaccustomed triumph, I could only sleep that night of June 26 for a few hours. As I lay awake, I praised God, murmuring the chorus of our family's favorite hymn:

"Glory! Glory! Alleluia! God's truth is marching on."

Tools to Help You Surrender

1. Remember to remember.
2. "Whatever may happen to me,
   Blessed be the name of Thee." (Author's poem)
3. "God grant me the serenity
   To accept the things I cannot change
   Courage to change the things I can
   And wisdom to know the difference." (Reinhold Niebuhr)
4. Surrender this present moment.
5. The road to transcending is through surrendering.
6. "Will to will the will of God." (Madame Pahk)
7. Surrender yourself to God, moment by moment, seeking
   the state of abandonment to God as a way of life.
8. Open wide your gates with thanksgiving.
9. Fiat voluntas tua. ("Thy will be done." Matthew 6:10)

Chapter 7

You Can Only Keep
What You Give Away

One of my best friends in prayer, Barney Lenahan, congratulated me on the citizenship victory but warned at the same time:

> Now, Susan, you've got to get used to freedom all over again. Remember you're just like a prisoner who has been sprung after a long time inside.

He should know; he was assistant sheriff of Broward County down here in Florida. I found adjusting to my new freedom a marvelous new and different experience. For now I was free from the long threat to my survival, permanent exile; free from the continued harassments of interrogations, subpoenas. And now I had been restored to freedoms Americans take for granted—the right to live and work where I wanted, the right to the vote that Aunt Susan had won, but I had lost. I could even now, if I wished, speak openly on political issues, the war, poverty, and women's rights.

I soon learned that my captivity in the cold war had paralyzed one whole half of my nature, the political animal in me. And we humans are both political animals, meant to take part in community life, and contemplative animals, reaching for oneness with God. During my long political stasis, God had activated the contemplative faculties, giving me some clarity on the end and means of human life as it is ordered to Him. And the end or goal of human life is, of course, the unitive state, union with Him, and union with our brothers and sisters on earth.

I had called the end and means "breakthrough" since 1960. It meant to me uniting your will to God's will, and uniting your life with that of your neighbor by love-in-action. Breakthrough seeks the Kingdom of God on earth as it is in heaven, not just for the individual, but for all sojourners on the planet. This high goal requires not just surrender, not just carrying the message; it requires the fifth and greatest freedom, freedom from self. This was a stumbling block not only to me, but, according to Evelyn Underhill, it was difficult even for the saints. She put it first when she wrote:

> What is a saint? A particular individual completely redeemed from self-occupation. . .

I meditated on this first part of her definition as I drove during the first days after victory to carry my personal thanksgivings to prayer groups that had kept prayer watch with me in Miami, Coral Gables, Palm Beach, and Pompano. I also meditated on a verse from the prophet Isaiah that told me to "proclaim a year of the Lord's favor. . . ." I would dedicate this year to thanksgiving, first in the letters, hundreds of them, that my students helped me address and stamp to the "team captains" of the prayer watch from Cutler, Maine, to Seattle, Washington; from Fort Worth to South Bend.

To proclaim a year of the Lord's favor also meant dedicating the twelve months ahead to trying once more to live up to that first charismatic prayer-poem:

Every minute I've spent on me,
Lord, I now dedicate to Thee.

But how? How would I dedicate this year to the Lord? Would writing the book be for Him, or would it be just my own ego trip? So many times that poor book had been interrupted in the sheer battle for survival. Now *God* had given me freedom politically, but I lacked the economic freedom to complete the book. I was submerged under the high legal fees and costs of the case, plus phone bills and ordinary living expenses. Not only did I lack my teaching salary, but I didn't have a penny coming in from anywhere. My many press and television interviews before and after victory had been given free, of course.

I tried to hand over the financial problem to the Lord with my new tool of surrender during the massive task of writing the thank-you letters. On the fourth day after victory, Catherine Marshall called me from Virginia. She was meeting at her mother's farm with some brand new publishers, all friends and colleagues on *Guideposts* magazine. They wanted me, after her glowing presentation, to send my manuscript up to them, and to follow it for a conference later.

Surely this was the green light from the Lord that it was His will for me to do what I so wanted to do, write the book. But delay set in and I began to waver, until the momentous day when Father Putz directed me to write the book full time, showing his faith in me as a writer by offering me a loan on which to start. Five months later the publishers gave me a contract and an advance. It was indeed a year of the Lord's favor. At the age of fifty-three, I had been given the writer's dream, the first chance in my entire life to sit down and write full time without the necessity of taking any other job. Every morning I joyfully went to my typewriter after my prayer period, seven days a week for nearly twelve months. As I sat there working steadily, I praised the Lord for this privilege, the truest happiness for a writer. It had been my father's goal every day of his life. But instead he had been forced always to report to his bread-and-butter job, giving only his exhausted nighttime hours to his plays and his magazine. Somehow I felt I was vindicating all his literary efforts. The year of the Lord's favor even extended to my legal debts. The lawyers offered to wait while I nibbled away at the costs month by month; they delayed in presenting their legal bill.

My cup seemed to be running over at the altar on Easter Sunday, 1970. It was one of the few times that I had actually felt the Lord's presence when receiving the Host. The words came to me:

"This Communion could be my spiritual marriage to Jesus Christ, the union I have sought all these years."

The next morning instead of going directly to my typewriter I was impelled to get in the car and drive to a jeweler to buy a pledge, a seal of my spiritual marriage, a plain gold wedding ring. The astonished jeweler measured my ring finger, no doubt wondering what was a middle-aged lady doing buying her own wedding ring? Surely if she were really getting married the groom would be with her buying the ring. He, of course, could not see the Bridegroom standing beside me. True I was overage for marriage to Him. But then I had come to love Him late. I had only met him ten years earlier when I was already in my forties. I walked out of the shop enjoying *"the high spirits peculiar to high spirituality."* (Italics mine.) I actually thought I had attained the high goal, union with God, that I had reached the top of the spiral stairway.

My high-flown presumption went crashing a few months later. I saw how far I had to climb when I went through the divorce trial ending my ten years of separation from Jack Lewis. During his denunciation of me in the court room, I asked myself, Where now was the interior peace I thought I had gotten? When I was stripped of our plantation, Rose Hill, now worth three million dollars, I walked out of the courthouse utterly flattened out. Back in Florida, nursing my wounds, I found strength and words to write Father Putz of the shocking loss of my expected half of the plantation that I had owned. Father Putz sent me words that I drank in for sheer survival:

> I received your letter this morning acquainting me of one more series of disappointments. The peeling-off process is continuing and I know that this is hard and cruel, yet in the long run, I am sure it will work in your spiritual advancement. Soon you will completely be your own person without any physical attachment to the past. God is asking this sacrifice for the good of the message that you have to preach to the poor of today's world. And the poor are less the physically deprived, but the spiritually deprived. Your own stripping of all material supports seems to be the condition of the effect of your gospel. . .It is people like X [a friend recently stripped of great wealth (AU.)] that you are help-

ing by your willingness to live the life of the poor [deprived of material resources] so that they can better take deprivation when it hits them. . .

Your greatest resources are not in the area of material goods now, but in the area of your spiritual power and strength. God is asking you that you put your trust in Him to the extent of leaving your future entirely in His hands. This is not easy, it is an immense act of faith, but it is the price of spiritual fruitfulness. Christ had no place to lay his weary head. Your commitment to the Gospel makes this a condition of discipleship. Religious life [i.e., in convents, etc. (AU.)] is really an escape from Christianity when you think of the hardships endured by most people totally dependent on their own resources and the charity of their fellowman.

Your next book must be on the mystery of suffering as experienced by someone in the world-marriage-politics-religious-economic-deprivation. What does this do to the human person? I think that your experience should be of help to others. You can be completely open and honest in the account since you have been sheared of all connections. Think about it. This is modern reality.

I clung to his letter in the winter of continued poverty, 1971, made worse now by the removal of my great expectations. The publication of my book was postponed three times, thus postponing the salability of articles to magazines and the new book I was trying to work on. But far more dreadful than poverty was the sudden eclipse of God.

Through my captivity I had not doubted the presence of God, since my conversion to Jesus. Now I could no longer see His face. My cottage, *Casa de la Paloma*, which had been like a house of prayer, now became a "den of thieves"—the interior thieves of self-occupation, of fear, frustration, and resentment, which robbed me of a treasure far greater than that of mere property and its cash value. For these thieves robbed me of God Himself. My prayers dried up. My health declined. I was, I at last realized, in the real dark night of the soul, the interior death of the self so much more shattering than the dark night of the senses. The life of my spirit had departed, just as He had, it seemed, left my little house, abandoning me to bitter loneliness for the first time since I had met Him, eleven years earlier in the San Diego YWCA.

True to my own teaching, I went through the motions of praying and meditating. Even though I could sometimes only say with Mary Magdalene, ". . .They have taken away my Lord, and I know not where they have laid him" (John 20:13), I held on to the survival tool that it was not my *feeling* of faith that mattered, it was only my *will to believe,* and to act as if I believed. The Body of Christ in the Church, the Sacraments, the prayer community remained my support, even though they did little to lift me up in my emotions. I kept my will directed toward God even though my heart was like stone.

I tried to turn my own suffering into sacrifice for the world's sufferers, particularly those in my own circle, my own prayer community. From morning till night they called for help from me, when I had so little to give. Their very pleas, however, redeemed me from my self-concern for the minutes, hours, and

143

days I spent on their problems.

Their needs reminded me that the previous year, 1969-1970, I had supposedly dedicated to the Lord as thanksgiving for my freedom. I had often shut off my phone as well as my ears. I had done this for the months that I slaved to finish my book, *The Ghost in My Life*. I had thought I was doing the will of God by limiting my activities, my work for others, to complete the book He had told me to write. Had I been instead living in a false paradise? Had I forgotten that *the price of spiritual maturity is spiritual maternity?* Had I forgotten that the price is to generate new children of the spirit all of the time, not just at the times when it is convenient to me? Had I forgotten the rule that had come to me so clearly from Him: *give all the while that you live?*

I searched the Gospels and found His own words, "I came not to be served, but to serve" (Matthew 20:28). I had said those words and even practiced them in the years, now decades, that I had helped my fellow alcoholics and other sufferers. But last year while writing the book I had withdrawn from all but the most essential service to others. I had turned down scores of invitations to speak to sufferers in groups. My rationalization had been, or course, my deadline on the book for the publishers.

I remembered the words of St. John of the Cross, "When the evening of this life comes, we shall be judged on Love."

I pondered the words given by Baron Von Hugel in which he, the great intellectual, summed up the life of the spirit:

"Caring matters most."

From Jesus on down through his saints in every

century the lesson hammered home, *you can only keep what you give away.* The survival tools all rust and become useless if you do not hand them out as soon as you receive them. Jesus is never reported in his public ministry as having refused a sufferer. He never said, "Don't bother me, I am too busy preaching the Gospel to help you." Rather did he heal and help each one who came to him—the sick, the blind, the woman about to be stoned to death for adultery. He retired to the mountain or desert to pray to the Father, only to return to the market place to heal, rescue, and redeem. Jesus did not lock himself up in a monastery or a study or a studio and shut out the sufferers. And he commanded us very strongly at the Last Supper: ". . .Love one another, as I have loved you" (John 15:12). And by every word and deed of his life he meant not love-in-dreams, but love-in-action. "I have chosen you and have appointed you that *you should go and bear fruit* [italics mine], and that your fruit should remain" (John 15:16).

In His very first sermon to his neighbors in Galilee He quoted the words of the prophet Isaiah, giving the content and purpose of His own brief mission on earth:

> The Spirit of the Lord is upon me,
> because he has anointed me to
> preach good news to the poor.
> He has sent me to proclaim release
> to the captives
> and recovering of sight to the blind,
> to set at liberty those who are oppressed,
> to proclaim the acceptable year of the Lord.
> (Luke 4:18,19)

145

Nor did He die for us so that we would limit ourselves to talking and writing about Him. He "died to make men holy," the old hymn says. "Let us die to make men free" ("The Battle Hymn of the Republic," *Atlantic,* February, 1862). Free of suffering, free of "mysterious downward drag within the world, which we call sin," as Evelyn Underhill puts it.

For what after all is a saint? Was a saint simply what William James had said in his book that I had found those many years ago on a mountain in Jamaica, a "character for which spiritual emotions are the habitual centre of the personal energy"? Or was a saint really one who followed in His steps, one described by Miss Underhill as, "A particular individual completely redeemed from self-occupation. . ."

We will never get to heaven alone. And on earth if we are to enter His kingdom—we must become saints not for our personal salvation alone; *we must become saints for the common good,* for the collective salvation of our brothers and sisters, and for their survival too.

St. Paul phrased the goal of Christian sanctity, ". . .I live, yet not I, but Christ does live in me" (Galatians 2:20). But he did not then hide himself in the desert or in the temple to savour his tasting knowledge of God. He never took a day's rest, and he even worked at night to support himself. He traveled more than any of the Apostles, pouring himself out to build the Kingdom of God on earth.

St. Catherine of Sienna abandoned her preferred solitary contemplation to become a saint for the common good in the political arena, to rescue the Pope from exile. The young girl who dreamed dreams left her solitary "cell of self-knowledge" to become an activist in solidarity with her fellow Christians. Joan of Arc was a saint not only in the visions of God, and the Virgin, but in her practical leadership of her fellow soldiers. My beloved Spanish saints, Teresa of Avila and John of the Cross, left their cloisters to launch ardent, activist reforms of their moribund, slack Carmelite order, a mission that took Teresa traveling on the back of a donkey throughout her rugged country.

And right in our own century, we have men and women of that thin, bright stream of saints for the common good. Dorothy Day was a woman in a hand-me-down dress, who held rapt the undergraduates and faculty at the University of Notre Dame, and led me to empty my purse for her cause. The cause of this holy woman was to help the poor, the unemployed through her soup kitchens, houses, and her newspaper, the *Catholic Worker*. She is high in my gallery of saints who take in from God so that they may give out to their fellow man. Utterly convinced, she convinced others who heard her that you can only keep what you give away; you can only give away what you have, and what you have comes only from uniting with God in prayer and action. She was a concerned contemplative for social change.

One man who puts to shame any of us who say, "I'm too busy to pray," was Dag Hammarskjöld. He carried not only the peace of the world on his slim shoulders as secretary-general of the United Nations, but he led an intense prayer life. He flew to his death on a mission for the common good, peace in Africa. It was only after he died that we learned the public peacemaker had spent his few solitary hours composing prayers to God in prose and in verse. The publication of *Markings* (Knopf, 1964) after his death revealed to us one more saint for the common good who combined contemplation with action.

My spiritual mother, Evelyn Underhill, led millions of us to Christ and the journey of the spirit through her written works. Physically frail, she poured herself out also through the hundreds of letters of spiritual direction she wrote personally to her children of the spirit. An ardent pacifist, she further taxed her strength in endless efforts with others to get the nations to disarm, to prevent World War II, spending herself in her final illness to write words of guidance and comfort to her children of the spirit.

More recently a short, roly-poly octagenarian moved the entire world by the power of the spirit of love operating through him. Pope John XXIII gave himself on a planetary scale, climaxed by his handiwork, Vatican II, that ushered in the age of ecumenism and opened the doors of his own church to the suffering of the modern world. His masterpieces, *Peace on Earth* and *Mother and Teacher*, are blueprints for the Kingdom of God on earth, fruit of his concern for the common good.

One frail little dark-skinned Hindu has been acclaimed the leading Christ-man of our century, even though he was, of course, not a Christian. He was called a Christ-man because he more than any Christian in our time demonstrated concretely in day-to-day political action Jesus Christ's teaching of nonviolence. He wrote, "Prayer. . .properly understood and applied. . .is the most potent instrument of action" (*Gandhi on Non-Violence*, New Directions, 1965). Achieving his own holiness through prayer and fasting was not enough for Gandhi. He gave everything of himself to free the oppressed, starving untouchables of India. He accomplished his unparalleled triumph through his charismatic leadership based on prayer and sacrifice. Despite the provocations and temptations assailing him, he held his people to the practice of nonviolence, leading them to freedom, until he was murdered by the assassin's bullet.

Then there is the suffering saint for the common good who, through his masterpiece and other books, survives today the punishment, exile, and harassment by the Catholic church he loved so well. Teilhard de Chardin, the mystic-scientist, was a prophet without honor in his own church, but with high honor among the leading thinkers of his century. Since his death he has been belatedly recognized by some Roman Catholic leaders. Endowed by the spirit with the gift of prophecy as well as contemplation, he gave us a vision of evolutionary convergence, of hope that we are going somewhere. He drew the scales off the eyes of millions of people who have read his works and the students and colleagues he knew in person, showing them the urgent necessity to love that which is created, as well as the Creator. He broke down the false barriers between spirit and matter, so that they should be down permanently in the minds of all who read him. More than that, he "Christified" evolution and in so doing Christified the natural as well as the supernatural goal of mankind.

Each of these men and women exemplified a balance between personal union with God, and collective union with the people of the world. Not one hid himself in a corner hugging his contemplative gifts to himself. But each, in the tradition of Jesus, spent his allotted time building the Kingdom of God on earth as it is in Heaven. Despite the demands of their national and international calling, Gandhi, Evelyn Underhill, and Dorothy Day spent themselves equally in person-to-person rescue work. The holy Gandhi, twenty-four hours before his murder, had agreed to give his time to instruct personally the spiritual seeker, the foreign correspondent, Vincent Sheean. Evelyn Underhill never gave up pouring herself out in spiritual direction until death stopped her voice and pen. Dorothy Day gave herself prodigally in person-to-person work at an age when most men and women expect to be served, not to serve.

How far you and I can go in reaching the goal of the journey—union with God or the unitive state—depends first on the grace of God, and second on our cooperation with His grace in prayer and work. The survival kit tools should not only help you to cooperate with His grace, they should provide you with a *flexible rule of life to structure your days*, to remind yourself that you are going somewhere and how to get there. The seven steps of the interior life that I call breakthrough (see Chapter 3, page 62) form a part of this rule to be used one day at a time.

The master tool of prayer must dominate your daily rule. And with prayer you must combine person-to-person action for others, one day at a time. You should include in your rule a weekly prayer meeting with others who are consciously moving from the kinship of suffering, through survival, to sanctity. You'll need them and they'll need you, not only for survival, but for the greater goal of transcendence. You'll also need the larger fellowship, the corporate body, who worship in a temple, hall, or church.

Your personal rule grows out of your own station in life, married, single, religious, working or retired. It must fit your particular stage of growth. For example, the time you spend in prayer, attending to God, may be at first only five minutes. Later, it may build to half and hour or more. Now you may set aside only ten minutes a day to meditate upon the Scriptures. Later that may well seem far too meager. Prayer and cleansing, prayer and fellowship, prayer and works, these are the essentials of your rule, your survival kit for each day. You will not find your rule burdensome, because at each moment you have help, help given you by Jesus who in His own life moved from suffering, to survival, to transcendence. He gave us a rule that undergirds any we might form:

> . . .Seek ye first the kingdom of God, and His righteousness; and all these things shall be added unto you. (Matthew 6:33)

And you will also have the help of your brothers and sisters—if even two or three of you gather together in His name in one of the thousands of prayer-share groups and communities that are springing up across the planet today. You can *seek* the Kingdom as a solitary person, but you will only *find* the Kingdom, in solidarity united with other sojourners.

Tools to Help You Attain and
Maintain the Unitive State

1. "Every minute I've spent on me
   Lord, I now dedicate to Thee." (Author's poem)
2. Enjoy "the high spirits peculiar to high spirituality." (Evelyn Underhill, Mysticism)
3. The price of spiritual maturity is spiritual maternity.
4. Give all the while that you live.
5. "When the evening of this life comes, we shall be judged on love." (St. John of the Cross)
6. "Caring matters most." (Baron Friederich Von Hugel, Letters To a Niece, London, 1928, p. xliii)
7. ". . .Love one another as I have loved you." (John 15:12)
8. Practice love-in-action, not just love-in-dreams.
9. Be a saint for the common good.
10. Follow a flexible rule for your spiritual growth, one day at a time.
11. While making your own breakthrough, carry the message, person to person and to the wider community, practicing these principles in all your affairs, one day at a time. (Step 7, Breakthrough)
12. . . .Seek ye first the kingdom of God, and his righteousness; and all these things shall be added unto you." (Matthew 6:33)

Chapter 8

Each One Reach One

Wherever you are at this moment in the United States you are within easy traveling distance of a small group of people meeting to help each other survive and/or transcend some kind of suffering. The meeting may be in a living room, classroom, parish hall, the board room of a bank, or a restaurant.

I use the word "breakthrough" as the general term to describe these groups that began as far back as 1935 to help individuals make breakthroughs from what they were to what they wanted to be.

The pioneer of all breakthrough groups and each-one-reach-one groups in our century is Alcoholics Anonymous. It set the pattern for most of those who meet for survival and sharing in the mushrooming movements today.

A glance at our gallery of survivors in the last seven chapters shows that none of them tried to go it alone. Each had some kind of a group to help in survival or transcendence. Mme. Induk Pahk, who was fleeced by her one-time friend, survived through a prayer group and transcended on a retreat with other believers. Dorrie, the working wife, got in touch with several prayer groups the moment she learned she had cancer. Sarah Gainham made her final breakthrough on prayer through the small group meeting she attended, and later by the long-distance support of the prayer community. John Howard Griffin was nourished by two groups, his unusually close and loving wife and children, plus the kinship with his Trappist monk friends at Gethsemane. Martin, the power-driven executive-turned-teacher, made his breakthrough in a prayer group. Father Putz, a leader and founder of many small group movements within the Catholic church has been part of and led small groups within and around the church since being ordained a priest.

My own survival has been built on small groups with the each-one-reach-one practice, both a sharing-survival group and a prayer group. You can begin your breakthrough in either type of group. But the nonbeliever will naturally gravitate toward a group based on survival-sharing. You are helped where you hurt, whether you practice prayer or not. This has been proved by all the groups patterned after Alcoholics Anonymous, including those for young drug addicts; Neurotics Anonymous; Gamblers Anonymous; and scores of others. Members are bound by a kinship of common hurts and band together for sharing-survival leading to recovery.

Almost two thousand years ago Jesus gave us the model for the small prayer-share group, as well as the survival kit for personal growth. He founded his breakthrough group, the community of twelve apostles, at the outset of his ministry. He drew together twelve ordinary men by his contagious love, and they demonstrated the leaven of the group in that they made their own breakthroughs from their personal inadequacies and hurts while helping others. Each, except the betrayer, went out and founded other groups that proliferated after Pentecost into the early church meetings in homes, praying and breaking bread together, and extending from Jerusalem onto the "end of the earth" as commanded by Jesus.

Originally these small groups met not only to worship God, but to help each man and woman in the group. They were true fellowships of love. But when the young church became a great hierarchical empire, the little community of Christians got lost in the growth. The more ardent fled to form their own communities, monasteries, and convents. The first of these, founded by St. Benedict, set the ideal group size for living and work at twelve, copying Christ's original group. Meanwhile, the church had begun putting protection of the institution of the church and the state, the power structure, before protection and growth of the individual. There was no place for the small group of Christians, until the revivals of other forms of Christianity took place, centering on the individual. But it was not until the twentieth century that the small group revolution began. And it is due perhaps to the fact that we now have the technological means, through transportation and communication, to make this growth possible.

Whatever your problem may be at this moment of reading, there is a breakthrough group available to help you at any stage you might be in toward survival or transcendence, ranging from the bottom—for suicide prevention—on up to the group dedicated to contemplation.

You can be as young as the eighth graders meeting in a rap group in a Connecticut junior high school, or as old as an octagenarian meeting in an inner city church with hippies who are also lonely. There is a place for you right now. You can now find the group you need through your church, local Crisis Line,

mental health center, or societies for specific problems or diseases.

The small group revolution has come to light only
recently in the popular media, perhaps because the
pioneers in the movement were strictly anonymous
members of AA. They were pledged not only to personal privacy at the level of press, radio, or television, but also restrained voluntarily from promoting
the program of AA. And since names make news, and
no names of living AA members are permitted to be
publicized, there has been little fanfare about this
historic movement. Yet witnessing, word of mouth,
and example have carried the small group therapy
message so that it is practiced for personal psychological breakthrough, or for encounter and sensitivity
sessions, and even for the more political rap groups
for black and women's rights.

Two so-called hopeless alcoholics began the whole
small group revolution. They were a broken down
stockbroker and a nearly dying doctor. Bill Wilson
and Dr. Bob, the cofounders of Alcoholics
Anonymous, found that, by leaning on each other
and rescuing other alcoholics, the miracle happened,
when "two or three are gathered together." They
found that each-one-reach-one works on the "incurable" disease of alcoholism. They found that you
can only keep what you give away, in this case,
sobriety. Out of their experience grew the fellowship
of AA that today has more than one million sober,
active members in 140 countries across the globe.

In literally thousands of meetings each week,
alcoholics come together to "share their experience,
strength and hope with each other that they may
solve their common problem and help others to

recover from alcoholism."

The early AA's wrote down in their "Big Book," called *Alcoholics Anonymous,* how the program works. A dozen years later, in 1951, the American Public Health Association gave AA the Lasker Award in recognition of its work with these prophetic words:

Historians may one day recognize Alcoholics Anonymous to have been a great venture in social pioneering which forged a new instrument for social action; a new therapy based on the kinship of common suffering; one having a vast potential for the myriad other ills of mankind.

That prophecy has been realized in the multiplication of kinship groups formed to make breakthroughs from the "myriad ills of mankind." The seminal group, AA, bases its recovery program on three main principles:

1. You are helped where you hurt, if you admit the hurt.
2. Each one reach one in person-to-person rescue work.
3. You need the help of a power greater than yourself, God as you understand Him.

Bill and Dr. Bob launched a planetary network of AA groups who help people get sober and stay sober by practicing the Twelve Steps. These are now familiar to you who have read the earlier chapters because I have drawn from them for the survival kit and its tools, and the seven steps of breakthrough. These steps are simple enough for the foggiest hungover drunk to read, yet deep enough for a contemplative to ponder for years. Here they are:

The Twelve Steps

1. We admitted we were powerless over alcohol—that our lives had become unmanageable.
2. Came to believe that a Power greater than ourselves could restore us to sanity.
3. Made a decision to turn our will and our lives over to the care of God *as we understood Him.*
4. Made a searching and fearless moral inventory of ourselves.
5. Admitted to God, to ourselves, and to another human being the exact nature of our wrongs.
6. Were entirely ready to have God remove all these defects of character.
7. Humbly asked Him to remove our shortcomings.
8. Made a list of all persons we had harmed, and became willing to make amends to them all.
9. Made direct amends to such people wherever possible, except when to do so would injure them or others.
10. Continued to take personal inventory and when we were wrong promptly admitted it.
11. Sought through prayer and meditation to improve our conscious contact with God *as we understood Him,* praying only for knowledge of His will for us and the power to carry that out.
12. Having had a spiritual awakening as the result of these steps, we tried to carry this message to alcoholics, and to practice these principles in all our affairs. (Alcoholics Anonymous Publishing Inc., *Alcoholics Anonymous,* 1955)

The Twelve Steps are the survival tools of every AA. If you will look at them closely, you will see that they embody the classical stages of spiritual growth, though not in the same order as those Underhill gave and I presented in the first seven chapters. Here is how they line up with those interior stages:

AA Steps 1 and 2 equal admission of your powerlessness and your awakening to a power greater than yourself.

Step 3 equals surrender to God as you understand Him.

Steps 4 through 10 equal the cleansing or purgation stage.

Step 11 is the same as the prayer-meditation stage, but omits mention of contemplation, in which God prays in us.

Step 12 equals the unitive state; that is, if you practice these principles in all your affairs and carry the message to alcoholics, you would indeed arrive at this peak of spiritual growth.

The AA Twelve Steps build up to the crucial twelfth step which is the combination of unconditional love-in-action plus spiritual experience, plus practicing all the principles listed. The twelfth step is the life blood of AA therapy. Based on the each-one-reach-one principle, it is perhaps best known of all the steps. Just the mention of AA, and you get the picture instantly of a sober alcoholic at the bedside of a drunk at three o'clock in the morning. And this is a true picture, since person-to-person rescue work is the heart of the AA program. Answering twelfth-step calls are not only the means by which drunks start on their road to recovery, but are the chief means for AA's to keep their sobriety.

From the moment of their first twelfth-step calls, until the day they die, the new alcoholics, called either "babies" or "pigeons" are immersed in the atmosphere of love-in-action that seems to say, "I love you no matter who you are, what you have done, what you may do."

AA sponsors nurse the new babies around the clock, cleaning up after them when they vomit, making their beds, walking up and down with them to get them over their shakes. The babies who have been locked in loathing of themselves, their families, their employers, and their fellow workers, often get their first taste of what the unconditional love of God is like through this human love shown by AA's. At first they are usually suspicious and ask: "What are you getting out of this?" They are so soaked in the materialistic orientation of society, the hidden gimmick, the angle, that they can't really believe someone will care for them without monetary gain.

Sober AA's answer, "What we get out of it is our lives—our sobriety—by helping you. We are helping ourselves stay sober."

For sober AA's are escaping the prison of their own self-concern. They simply don't have time to think of themselves while giving themselves to others. Gone for the time being are their own self-pity, resentment, and frustration in their concern for the sick alcoholic. They remind themselves of this in a sentence written on the walls of most AA meeting halls:

"There but for the Grace of God go I."

They identify with the baby, knowing that they share the same inner nature. In this kinship of disease they know the effect that "cunning, baffling, powerful"alcoholism has had on the new man or woman.

They can say with complete authority:

"I know how you feel—I have been there myself."

Sharing is not limited to the bedside of the sick alcoholic coming off a binge. It is the basis of every AA meeting, whether the small discussion group or the much larger open meeting with one to three speakers. At the latter, AA's tell their own stories. They first qualify themselves as true alcoholics by telling how they hit bottom and then what AA has done for them.

The discussion groups, numbering from six to twenty-five, usually feature open-ended sharing on any of the Twelve Steps or the "props" which include:

> Live one day at a time.
> Stay away from the first drink.
> First things first.
> Easy does it.
> One step at a time.
> Keep it simple.

These discussions form the major group therapy of AA. Members drop their masks, their facades, and "ventilate" at depth. Meetings take place every night of the week in the larger cities. It is here at these meetings that the tools of the survival kit are given to each alcoholic to get sober and stay sober. Most AA's have a home group that they always attend once a week, no matter how many others they may go to. That home group becomes in some cases the first real family that alcoholics have known, a group in which they fit in and are accepted and can be completely themselves.

Talks or discussions almost always include the

spiritual growth aspect of AA. Though AA is not de-nominationally or institutionally religious, it is based on spiritual principles. The very basis for taking the first three steps is that only a power greater than yourself can restore you to sanity, and that you must at least be *willing* to surrender your life and your will to that power.

There are almost as many concepts of the power as there are AA's. Some consider it to be the group of sober AA members. Some think of it as the sea around them, or the universe. Many AA's experience a conversion or reconversion to a personal God. But at whatever stage of belief the members are, the talk at AA is always about interior growth. One Carmelite priest AA told me:

> I've heard more real discussion about God in AA meetings or over a cup of coffee with a fellow AA than in my twenty years living in the monastery.

The power of the group or personal God as each understands Him leads AA's through growth from sheer physical sobriety, or surface sobriety, to sobriety in depth which begins with sanity, goes on to serenity, and should any AA's ever practice all the Twelve Steps all the time, they would indeed reach sanctity. And whether the members are Christian, Jewish, Moslem, or pagan, they seem to follow this growth pattern. And they are never turned off by any brand of religion being forced on them because this is simply not condoned. Though the program embraces Christian principles, especially the distinctively Christian command to show love-in-action, not just love-in-dreams, the AA spiral stairway is not Christian in the theological or doctrinal sense. It is universal.

Alcoholics are primarily misplaced mystics with a tremendous thirst for God that they have slaked with substitutes such as fame, success, money, and the easiest way, alcohol. They can, once they join the program, become mature mystics, borne along by the leaven of the group in the growth process of the spirit. By admitting their powerlessness and surrendering to a higher power, they embark on a seven step cleansing-and-amends regime (steps four through ten) as demanding as any monk's mortification. They begin to pray and meditate as suggested in the eleventh step, to improve their "conscious contact with God" as they understand Him.

AA meetings open with a moment of silent meditation and most close with the Lord's Prayer. Most members who have been on the program even a few weeks start their mornings by reading a little book called *A Day at a Time*, or one called *Twenty-Four Hours a Day*, both geared to their need for spiritual reading and meditation. For those who want to go further in the spiritual life, there are special eleventh step meetings. Here members share their progress in prayer, methods of prayer, spiritual experiences, and sometimes pray together.

But all AA's, whether believers or not, recite "The Serenity Prayer." It is on the walls of meeting halls, plaques, cards, and written in the hearts of members. At many meetings it is used as an opening following the moment of silent meditation. Groups copying AA also use the prayer that was written, as mentioned in Chapter 6, by Reinhold Niebuhr. And it is an irony that despite all his more scholarly writings, he will be remembered best for this tiny yet efficacious prayer:

> God grant me the serenity
> To accept the things I cannot change
> Courage to change the things I can
> And wisdom to know the difference.

As a result of the intensive, daily concentration on interior growth as a means of survival, of staying away from a drink, there are probably more practicing mystics in AA than in any other fellowship in today's world. They would never call themselves mystics, but they demonstrate the marks of the mystic, including one basic one. There are just no barriers in AA among people of radically differing religions, races, creeds, and politics. AA in fact has pioneered as a convergent group, uniting, within its loose-structured, autonomous meetings, men and women who range from the extreme right to anarchists. Their convergence is a demonstration that a kinship born of common suffering can indeed transcend opposing ideologies.

I was impressed by this convergence when I had the privilege of attending AA's Thirty-fifth Anniversary World Convention at Miami Beach in the summer of 1970. At the session called "AA Round the World," I saw a white, blonde South African lady sharing a platform with a black Jamaican and a German sitting next to a Dane. They were obviously in complete accord. Love seemed to reach out from each to the other and to the vast audience. Though the apartheid policies of the South African government are certainly at the opposite pole from the complete integration of Jamaica, West Indies, and though the Dane had suffered from the occupation by the Germans in World War II, these speakers transcended all that. They simply represented themselves, recovered alcoholics who had helped each other survive. The white South African did not see the blackness of the Jamaican, nor did he object to her whiteness. The Dane seemed perfectly content to share the platform with the German. There were no labels on any of them. They loved each other as individuals. It is highly unlikely that, if they ever met on a battlefield or in a riot, this Jamaican could be induced to kill this South African, or that this German could be forced to kill this Dane.

The convergence was not limited to the speakers. Seated next to me in the audience was a high-ranking conservative law-and-order police officer. On his left was a long-haired, bearded hippie boy. In the same row was a rich white-haired retiree from Palm Beach whom I happened to know was as Birchite in his political views as the young boy was radical. Yet they merged as one, nodded in agreement to each other, smiled or grew tearful together at the stories told by the German, the Jamaican, the South African, and the Dane.

The AA preamble states, "AA is not allied with any sect, denomination, politics, organization or institution; does not wish to engage in any controversy; neither endorses or opposes any causes."

That is the tradition of AA and one that is adhered to. But beyond that the sword of that first drink ever hanging over the head serves to cool down the alcoholics' political differences. They may dislike the ideologies of the persons sitting on either side at the meetings, but those very same persons may be the only ones available to help them fight a drink should the craving come. Nor is there much sex discrimination in AA. Though men may still outnumber women in the fellowship, women are, in most cases, as welcome as men.

What is discouraged is love affairs between new AA's. This for the very good reason that if an AA woman transfers all her affection to an AA man, she will probably get drunk if he does, and vice versa. Women and men, blacks and whites, Jews and Christians, pagans and believers, Republicans and anarchists, AA members share not only their common suffering, but their common hope. And sharing a common hope for survival forms an equally important bond.

Had AA succeeded in only sobering up its own one million members it would still be worthy of its citation as a "great venture in social pioneering which forged a new instrument for social action." But the fact is that AA has generated thousands of breakthrough groups for other types of sufferers. The most publicized have been those to help young drug abusers recover, centers called The Turning Point, Spectrum House, The Seed, and hundreds of different names throughout the country. They range from the nonspiritually oriented groups and communes to the distinctively Christian "Teen Challenge Centers" founded by the Reverend David Wilkerson, author of the best-selling book from which a film was made, *The Cross and the Switchblade* (Bernard Geis, 1963).

Though Jesus was not mentioned specifically at the drug center The Seed in Fort Lauderdale, the word "love" dominated every testimony given by young people ranging from twelve to twenty-five years of age. More than twenty boys and girls ended their short talks with "I love you, Mom and Dad. I love you, group." All of the youngsters said they had started their drug careers on pot, every one of them. Most had graduated to psychedelics, uppers and downers, and then to cocaine or heroin. Some had been referred to The Seed by the courts, but most by their parents. The young people are required to live in foster homes with others who have been rehabilitated by the program. The Seed educates them to stay away from any and all mood changers, not just pot, but pills, booze, and uppers and downers.

Borrowing AA's structure of the small group, but not its content, are other kinds of therapy, sensitivity workshops, and encounter groups held in such settings as colleges, corporations, churches, and hotels. Unlike AA, these groups depend on human mind working on human mind. There is not a reliance on a power greater than themselves. They have certain similarities to the breakthrough groups I started in 1960, namely sharing and ventilating problems. But they do not suggest submission to a higher power. Interaction among individuals, not love-in-action, seems to be the prescribed method, according to graduates of both sensitivity and encounter groups. Though they borrow the form of the AA small discussion group, they tend to leave out the spirit of God and/or the spirit of unconditional love. In fact, one graduate has told me that a fearful neurotic person has a difficult time surviving hostile encounter groups or even the milder touch-and-tell games played to break down reserve.

Insight from one's own subconscious, not revelation from God, is sought in the groups. The positive results come to participants in greater awareness. One friend told me she had learned a great deal about herself in an encounter group during a training period for drug rehabilitation:

> The concentrated onslaught of the group, telling me I was defensive in almost everything I said, shook me up. I began to review my whole life. I found that I had indeed been defending everything I had been doing with my husband, my children, my job, my views. I learned out there that I do not have to be on the defensive. I am trying to change.

Though these groups help people survive in some cases, they help participants *transcend* suffering only accidentally. And despite the pioneering of AA in making this the century of the small group, there still remained the need for the step beyond sharing and survival. That need, for transcending suffering, is being met partially by the renewal and growth of the prayer group movement among all denominations. These groups could be called kinships of *dedication*, as distinct from the kinships of *difficulty* that began with AA. Prayer groups are based not only on a common hope, but on a common faith that God himself, not just an impersonal power greater than yourself, will lead you to transcend and transmute suffering.

*   *   *   *   *   *   *   *

I had a dream back on the hillside at Rose Hill in Jamaica. My dream was the old hope of humanity, "to know the truth about God and to live in communities" (St. Thomas Aquinas). So we set about building a chapel that would be the center of a house of prayer on our plantation. It was only a half-finished skeleton when I had to leave Rose Hill. But I still have that dream—a dream that somewhere, some day I may live in a house of prayer with non-alcoholics as well as recovered alcoholics, who want to go all the way to union with God using the steps and tools described in this book.

In this house we will pray for the survival and transcendence of each suffering person who needs our prayer. And we will also pray, as I do each day, for our suffering society. We will pray that it may become a society that renders contemplation possible for *all* its members, not just a spiritual elite—a society, as Dorothy Day said, in which it would be "easier to be good." We would seek to remove obstacles within ourselves that bar our way to union with goodness, union with God.

An eighteenth century English writer William Law wrote:

Nothing hath separated us from God but our own will, or rather our own will is our separation from God. All the disorder and corruption and malady of our nature lies in a certain fixedness of our own will, imagination and desire, wherein we live to ourselves, are our own centre and circumference, act wholly from ourselves, according to our own will, imagination and desires.

Some of you are blessed with a total surrender to God and your will dissolves in your generous gift of your will to Him. Others, and I include myself among them, are still painfully aware of the "fixedness of our own will." When I remember to remember, I try to *act* as though I were already surrendered to God's will, to *act* as though I am already in union with Him. I take on this new self as though I were a "method" actress, one who acts from the inside out. How did it feel the last time I actually was one with Him, when I walked with Him on the beach, or in the forest, or gave my time and energy to caring for an alcoholic? Then I try to capture that feeling and to "act my way into right thinking."

Too often I slip back into "I want what I want when I want it," instead of "I will to will the will of God." Yet even when we give up and think we are moving farther and farther from union with God, "something" happens. Then we realize that in spite of ourselves, we have committed a perfectly unselfish act. And then the angels sing and we rejoice and we are exceeding glad, for we have tasted, if only for a moment, what St. Paul meant when he said:

". . . It is no longer I who live, but Christ who lives in me."

Galatians 2:20

About the Author

Susan B. Anthony is the spirited grandniece and namesake of the famous nineteenth century champion of women's rights. In her busy lifetime, she has been an educator and an alcoholic, an item in New York gossip columns and a journalist, an ordained minister and a Catholic convert, a pioneering feminist and a theologian, a political victim and an alcoholism counselor. Out of these disparate roles, she has emerged with a spiritual wholeness that has inspired thousands on her country-wide speaking tours.

Like her great-aunt, she has energy, conviction, and a habit of flinging herself wholeheartedly into what she does and what she believes.

The nineteenth century Susan declared staunchly that "failure is impossible." The twentieth century Susan, who has transcended more than her fair share of suffering, believes that too. She survived a series of storms in her personal life that threatened to sweep her to disaster.

Alcoholism blurred her college years and her early career in journalism and broadcasting. As a young reporter caught in the maelstrom of history, she was viciously victimized during the McCarthy era and struggled to retain her citizenship. Three marriages collapsed in divorce. And over all of these troubles hovered the ghost of the first Susan. In her autobiography, *The Ghost in My Life*, the second Susan talks about coming to terms with this powerful ancestral presence.

A magna cum laude graduate of the University of Rochester, Dr. Anthony holds a bouquet of degrees: two M.A.s, in political science and theology; a Ph. D. in theology from Saint Mary's college, Notre Dame, Indiana (she was among the first fifteen lay women to earn this degree); and an honorary degree (doctor of letters) from St. Mary-of-the-Woods College, Indiana.

She is the author of seven books and has been a reporter for the *Washington Star* and Florida newspapers, an Associated Press correspondent, and a contributor to national magazines and newspapers.

Her professional service to alcoholics began with an innovative radio program in Boston in 1949. In 1976, after thirty years of sobriety, she was honored at a U.S. Senate reception for her work with women and alcoholism. Since that time, she has contributed her expertise in these areas to national and international policy-making conferences and has traveled 500,000 miles to eighty-five cities, lecturing, consulting, and holding spiritual retreats.

In Florida, she coordinated and counseled in a substance abuse program in south Palm Beach County and co-founded Wayside House, a residential center for recovering alcoholic women.

Dr. Anthony is now in private practice in South Florida, counseling alcoholics and their families. She lives in Deerfield Beach, just a block from the sea, where she swims, snorkels, and takes daily meditation walks along the shore.

Her life and work today bring together her three major commitments—to God, to human freedom, and to recovery from alcoholism for those still suffering.

Other CompCare Books
That Offer Comfort and Courage

A Day at a Time. This familiar, pocket-size CompCare classic, with its rust cover and gold title, now has a quarter of a million copies in print. These daily readings—thoughts, prayers, and memorable phrases for coping with life's complexities—are helpful for anyone, but especially for those working Twelve-Step Programs. Its wise words are passwords to serenity for the thousands who have made this little book a bedside or a carry-along source of strength. For gifts, sobriety anniversaries, other special moments, choose the deluxe cover in padded burgundy leather-grained vinyl. *Hard cover.*

The Conquering Spirit by Carol Hegarty. This serene little book brings comfort to anyone who is grieving over a death, divorce, or any kind of loss. It points out the solace that can come through human sharing and awareness of "the perfect circle of nature." The author's own wisdom is accompanied by tranquil photographs and classic quotations. Counselors, ministers, friends find this booklet a gentle way to reaffirm life for those who are bereaved, without masking or minimizing their sorrow. *Quality paperback.*

Consider the Alternative by Lee M. Silverstein. The author-therapist, known nationally for his inspiring lectures and workshops, shares his personal story of recovery and synthesizes popular helping theories into a practical guide for living. This beautiful blend of humanity and therapy has been greeted with enthusiasm by experts Albert Ellis, Joel Fort, William Glasser, John Powell, and Sidney B. Simon, who wrote the foreword. *Quality paperback.*

Love Is a Hunger by Earnest Larsen. A counselor and author of over thirty books on human relations and spirituality (including *Godseekers* and *Good Old Plastic Jesus*) takes us on a pleasant, poetic saunter through some of the most basic and often ignored principles which make for a happy love relationship. This is not only an excellent guide for anyone who would like to be a more loving person, but an invaluable resource for marriage counselors. *Illustrated quality paperback.*

This Will Drive You Sane by Bill L. Little. Foreword by Albert Ellis. A warm-hearted therapist with a towering sense of humor, known for his on-the-air counseling sessions over CBS Radio KMOX out of St. Louis, backhandedly shows how to *get rid of* problems by explaining, in droll detail, how to *produce* them. Misery is not simply a state of being, but an art to be developed—and wallowed in! This humorous approach to everyday problems can ease stress and provide a healthy perspective. *Quality paperback.*

The Twelve Steps for Everyone. . .who really wants them. Originally written to interpret the Program of Alcoholics Anonymous for members of Emotional Health Anonymous (EHA), this sensitive book can help anyone find strength and healing through AA's Twelve Steps. Individuals and groups find this interpretation of the Twelve Steps—now with 125,000 in print—easy to understand and apply to their own lives. *Quality paperback.*

All of the above books are published by and available from CompCare Publications. None is either endorsed or opposed by the author of this book. Ask us to send you a free CompCare Publications catalog of quality books and other materials emphasizing a positive approach to life's problems for young people and adults on a broad range of topics. If you have questions, call us toll free at 800/328-3330. (Minnesota residents: Call 612/559-4800.)

2415 Annapolis Lane, Suite 140, Minneapolis, Minnesota 55441
A division of Comprehensive Care Corporation